THE *COMPLETE* *REFERENCE* *CHECKING* *HANDBOOK*

SECOND EDITION

THE COMPLETE REFERENCE CHECKING HANDBOK

SECOND EDITION

The Proven (and Legal) Way
to Prevent Hiring Mistakes

Edward C. Andler
with Dara Herbst

AMACOM
American Management Association
New York • Atlanta • Brussels • Buenos Aires • Chicago • London • Mexico City
San Francisco • Shanghai • Tokyo • Toronto • Washington, D.C.

This publication is designed to provide accurate and authoritative information in regard to the subject matter covered. It is sold with the understanding that the publisher is not engaged in rendering legal, accounting, or other professional service. If legal advice or other expert assistance is required, the services of a competent professional person should be sought.

Library of Congress Cataloging-in-Publication Data

Andler, Edward C.
    The complete reference checking handbook : the proven (and legal) way to prevent hiring mistakes / Edward C. Andler, Dara Herbst.—2nd ed.
        p.   cm.
    Includes index.
    ISBN 0-8144-0744-7 (hardcover)
    1. Employee screening—United States.   2. Employee selection—United States.   3. Employment references—United States.   I. Herbst, Dara, 1961–   II. Title.

HF5549.5.E429   A53   2002
658.3'112—dc21

                                                                2002009374

Printing number

10   9   8   7   6   5   4   3   2   1

To all the good employers who are being hurt because they haven't exercised due diligence regarding those they hire.

Contents

Acknowledgments

WE WOULD LIKE TO THANK our clients, our seminar partici-pants, and also the many references we have spoken with for their support and ideas on the subject of background screening. Through these contacts we have used and re-fined our practices and techniques in order to be success-ful in this area. They have allowed us to test our theories and thinking in the real world.

We would especially like to thank our families, who have given us the time and space to pursue our profes-sion. Our work often requires calling after normal busi-ness hours and on weekends, which has sometimes interfered with previously planned activities.

We would like to acknowledge the valuable editorial guidance of AMACOM Books, in particular from Adri-enne Hickey, executive editor, and Erika Spelman, associ-ate editor. Their creative suggestions were immensely helpful.

Also, our special thanks to Lois Vander Waerdt, J.D., and her firm, The Employment Partnership, for her con-tinuing legal guidance and ongoing encouragement.

THE COMPLETE
REFERENCE
CHECKING
HANDBOOK

SECOND EDITION

Introduction

BECAUSE OF THE TERRORIST EVENTS in 2001, more employers are now conducting background checks, fingerprinting new hires, and stepping up security measures that go well beyond what they have been doing in the past, if in fact, they were doing any type of checking at all. Trucking companies are lobbying Congress to give them full access to nationwide criminal databases to check the background of drivers. Airport officials are calling for the fingerprinting of all employees. And a push is on to make it easier for private energy companies to carry out criminal background checks on all their workers.

More companies, not only those in security-sensitive industries, are checking out employees because they want their clients and other employees to feel safe. However, companies may find themselves facing new hurdles in their rush to check workers. For example, the Fair Credit Reporting Act has specific guidelines that employers must now follow when checking out a potential employee's background when using a third party to provide them with information. In addition, checking out a person's criminal history can be a complicated and time-consuming process because the laws regarding information released vary in all fifty states.

1

Many companies are not aware of the obstacles they will face when conducting a background check on an individual, which is why we have written this book. We want to provide help and guidance in a misunderstood area so that companies will avoid legal and regulatory difficulties.

A MAJOR PROBLEM

Smart hiring is one of the primary factors in remaining competitive and successful in today's business world. Hiring the wrong employees results in high turnover, absenteeism, undesirable behavior, and theft on the payroll—with considerable cost consequences to the company. Each year, many U.S. organizations spend a considerable amount of time, money, and energy on newly hired employees who do not work out and either leave on their own or are fired. If employers had spent a little extra time and effort up front—and spoken with people who knew or worked with these applicants—far fewer bad hiring decisions would have been made.

For the hiring manager or supervisor responsible for making employment decisions, hiring the right people is the smart thing to do, and background checking is the key. Most applicants have not committed crimes. Most do not engage in substance abuse. Most do not distort their backgrounds—although an increasing number of résumés contain false information about unearned degrees, job titles, responsibilities, or salaries. If you do not thoroughly check out the people you are hiring, you are taking a tremendous risk and could face the liability of negligent hiring.

Whether an employer is hiring a minimum wage employee or a CEO, a thorough check is a crucial aspect of the hiring process.

WHY A SPECIAL BOOK ON REFERENCE CHECKING?

Our purpose in writing this book is simply to help you avoid major hiring mistakes. We focus on practical methods that help managers, supervisors, and professionals to improve their ability to conduct background checks on prospective employees.

This is not a book on personnel theory or legal interpretations. We focus on techniques and the reasons for including reference checking in your hiring decisions. We want to empower you to do a better job by providing you with new and powerful ideas that will enable you to immediately become more proficient in this area. We also show you why there is so much confusion and the fallacies surrounding background screening.

After reading this book, review your current thinking and practices regarding hiring, then combine them with these new ideas—and you will greatly enhance your chances of choosing the right person for each job you must fill. If you are not doing job-related reference checking as a routine part of your hiring process, it is time you started! If you are not cooperating with other employers when they call you for information about employees and former employees, it is time you reconsidered your policy.

We truly believe that in today's difficult times, no organization will be successful in assembling a strong workforce unless it turns to innovative, nontraditional strategies for selecting the best available workers.

FREQUENT QUESTIONS

Before proceeding, let's examine some frequently asked questions about reference and background checking:

Q. *What do the majority of companies research during an employee background check?*
A. A background check usually consists of confirmation of dates of employment with previous employers, confirmation of education, criminal record search, credit history, driving record check, and in some cases, an identity check is also undertaken.

   A reference check consists of speaking with previous supervisors and coworkers to determine whether the candidate has the requirements and skills for the job.

Q. *What kinds of employers conduct background checks, and how common are they?*
A. About half of all employers conduct some kind of background check before hiring workers, although the depth of the checks varies. Some workplaces, such as nuclear power plants, defense facilities, and other high-risk federal installations, have required extensive checks for decades. In the private sector, background probes occur in a vast range of industries, governed by individual company policies.

Q. *How many years back are you allowed to investigate?*
A. Federal law limits screenings to seven years. This means a criminal conviction a decade ago, for instance, cannot be included.

Q. *When is a background check illegal?*
A. An employer cannot target certain workers for background checks based on name, age, ethnic origin, or any other characteristic that would suggest illegal discrimination. An employer is safe conducting background checks on job candidates or on groups of employees who fit a certain job description. If the organization hires an outside company to conduct the

check, it is required by federal law to notify the person who is being investigated.

Q. *Isn't checking a person's reference mainly to see whether that person is lying?*
A. Checking for truthfulness is actually secondary to determining a candidate's past job performance and overall competence level.

Q. *Is asking a candidate to clarify unclear or confusing information that surfaced during the background check legally dangerous?*
A. Having the candidate clarify confusing information is really the only fair thing to do with someone you still consider a viable candidate.

We believe, when you finish this book, you will fully understand these observations.

Dishonesty—A Major Business and Social Problem

An Overall Look

A SURVEY CONDUCTED BY OUR firm in 2002 found that the higher the rank of the person being hired, the more likely the employer is to do a reference check. Eighty-three percent of employers always checked references for executive, administrative, or professional employees, whereas only 30 percent checked references for their hourly employees. Fifty-eight percent spoke to former employers or supervisors and 48 percent verified schools attended and degrees earned.

Survey respondents further indicated that they rarely received information about violent or bizarre behavior. They did, however, receive adequate information on the reason the applicant left his or her previous employer 41 percent of the time, on work habits (absence, tardiness, etc.) 40 percent of the time, and on serious personality traits 34 percent of the time.

THE PROBLEM

If you have not been checking out your employees before hiring them, you can assume that possibly one-third of the people working for you gained their jobs by creatively presenting their backgrounds and capabilities to your so-called hiring expert. The difficulties that human resources professionals face when checking references have only compounded deception and exaggeration by job candidates. This becomes an even bigger problem when the job market is tight and hiring is low. Many job seekers believe that they must "fluff up" the information on their résumés to be considered for the position and also to remain competitive in the job market.

Let's face it, when the information provided by a job applicant is not checked out and verified, you are providing an opportunity for questionable individuals to take advantage of the situation and lie. Even honest job seekers will eventually resort to falsification to keep up with the dishonest ones who are getting by on false pretenses.

The result is that when companies do not thoroughly check out candidates before they are hired, they continue exchanging the poor ones among themselves. When you stop to think about it, does it make sense to fire a poor employee and then turn right around and hire another bad one? Yet, when you fail to take the time to check out the candidates you hire, that is exactly what you are doing. When you hire someone else's problem, you are right back where you started. This is precisely why many companies are never able to upgrade their workforce.

Wouldn't it be nice to be able to spot these individuals yourself and not bring them on board? In our business of providing third-party reference-checking services for client companies, we have found that about 10 percent of the job candidates we check out are not hired because of information we uncover. When we report back to an employer that a candidate has falsified his or her background in some way, the employer is glad that the discrepancy was found before offering that person employment. We frequently hear comments like, "They obviously didn't think their references were actually going to be checked" or "Can you believe how many years he has been able to get by on that made-up degree?"

JOB MARKET DISTORTION

Let's look at how distortion occurs in the job market. Take the case of a fictional sales candidate (we will call him Tom) who, during the course of his career, has basically been an average performer. Wherever he was employed, Tom consistently ranked in the middle among the company's sales force at year's end. Some years he was a little above average; other years he was slightly below the middle mark. Tom had some very good months when he was near the top in sales and he also won a few special contests and opened a number of new accounts. However, over the long haul, the middle has been his place among the group. Tom is dissatisfied with his current employer and has decided to look for new employment. Tom knows he is a reliable but not an exceptional sales representative, so to present himself as a viable candidate, he "fluffs" his background when he goes out for interviews.

Tom exaggerates his past performance by telling a prospective employer that he was one of his company's best salespeople. Now, this is probably a fairly normal occurrence, and in Tom's case, this is not completely false because there were times when he was near the top in his sales performance. However, if you were to speak with his previous supervisors you would find that, overall, he was an average salesperson and would be able to make an informed hiring decision based on the truthful information you received from his references.

Now, let's say Tom tells an employer that he was singled out to train other sales representatives. This statement would lead you to believe that he is a very competent indi-

vidual and that he would probably be a tremendous addition to your sales force. Again, by speaking with his
previous supervisors and coworkers you would find out
that the entire sales force was brought in every Friday
morning for refresher training, and each sales representative was assigned various subjects on a routine basis to
cover for about an hour. He was not singled out for his
expertise but was merely used as a trainer, at times, as
a way to fulfill the training need. In this case Tom has
deliberately misrepresented his role, which we believe
you would agree is a much more serious distortion of the
facts.

Now, let's say Tom tells a potential employer that he
was in the top 10 percent of his company's sales force
last year, which is an outright lie. After speaking with his
references, you find that this was not the case and that
this is an obvious attempt to get you to believe that he is
something he is not.

In the first case of exaggeration, you may still hire
Tom, depending on how everything else looks. In the second instance, where there was obvious misrepresentation, you would most likely lose interest in him as a
candidate. And, in the third situation, where Tom lied to
you, you would definitely call it off.

The problem is that job seekers have learned from
previous job searches that the information they provided
was not checked, so they continue to lie, thinking they
will be able to get away with it again. In Tom's case, he
assumed the information he provided would not be verified and was caught lying.

THE BOTTOM LINE

What is the real effect of exaggeration, misrepresentation,
and lying by job candidates? As with buying any product
or service that is not what it was advertised to be, you are

not getting what you thought you were getting. A candidate eager for a job is under tremendous pressure and is likely to say whatever he or she thinks you want to hear to get the job. Finding out up front that candidates have either misrepresented themselves or do not have the skills or qualifications necessary for the job will save your company a great deal of time and money. Bad news usually costs a lot less when you get it sooner rather than later.

Over the years, we have spoken with hundreds of hiring managers who admit that they make hiring decisions without conducting a thorough background check on their applicants. They acknowledge that they are not getting the necessary information on work habits, past level of performance, human relations skills, personality traits, salary history, reason for leaving previous employers, and civil records.

Effective hiring means assessing all aspects of the job, carefully considering the applicants, and using available information to enhance the hiring decision. There is no law or requirement that job applicants must tell you their flaws—or even be truthful. It is the employer's task to find the distortions or lies.

It is a new age in hiring with new challenges for businesses to face and solve. For those of you responsible for ensuring that the wrong people are not hired, we have found that there are creative measures that can be taken, which we discuss in length throughout this book.

Initial Steps

IT IS NOW TIME TO regain control over the hiring process and to stop undesirable candidates from penetrating your workforce. Candidates can no longer be allowed to have the upper hand.

Candidates instinctively know that they are competing against other job seekers for a particular job. Depending on the position and the number of people competent and willing to fill it, the amount of competition varies. A candidate basically has to stand out from the other candidates to get the job. For all practical purposes, coming in second is no better than coming in last, because the bottom line is that they did not get the job. For many applicants, therefore, being successful means bending the facts to be the victor. Job applicants usually lie for the following two reasons:

1. To appear more competent and valuable to the company (create a higher compensation need)
2. To avoid discussing something that will lower their standing in the interviewer's opinion

IDENTIFY PROBLEM CANDIDATES

There are three basic types of problem candidates that employers must be able to spot during the hiring process:

1. *The underqualified.* Those who simply do not have the background, knowledge, or skills to be able to function in today's complex job categories.
2. *People who are burned out.* Those who have stayed in some job area too long and are tired and worn out. They need to get out of their old line of work and into something new.
3. *The emotionally unstable.* Those who are alcoholic, drug dependent, or subject to some intractable emotional problem.

A hiring mismatch is harmful in many ways. It takes a heavy psychic toll in stress and unhappiness on the individual, which can be transmitted to his or her family and friends. Certainly, other employees notice and feel the impact of someone who is not up to doing the job. In fact, they are the first to notice and to be affected by substandard job performance. Finally, employees who are not able or willing to do their jobs properly can seriously affect an employer's business image, productivity, and even profits.

The problem is that most candidates do not believe or want to believe that they are underqualified, burned out, or no longer emotionally fit for the type of work they are doing. Even when they have experienced troubles in their careers that clearly point to their not being well suited to their work, they continue to seek out jobs in the same line of work.

The first step in weeding out undesirable candidates

is to insist that the applicant provide all information requested on employment forms. The employment application and related forms are important documents and all blanks should be filled in properly before being accepted. An incomplete application may indicate that the applicant is careless or does not follow instructions well. Also, he or she may be trying to hide something.

The applicant is the logical source for information about himself. He knows the names of his former employers and supervisors. He should know, or can look up, the telephone numbers of past employers and references. This information is important to the verification process, and not providing it can make background checking a futile effort. Also, not having this information costs time and money when trying to complete the process.

When the company insists that all information be provided, a surprising number of applicants will eliminate themselves by not finishing the paperwork. They realize that the employer is serious and intends to check their full background. If someone has a reason for not wanting his or her references checked, or does not want a criminal, education, driving or credit check, he or she may simply not complete or return the required paperwork. Applicants usually know where they stand and how they will come out when checked on. Of course, all documents should always be signed when requested.

We suggest that someone be designated to review the application and other paperwork before it is accepted. All omitted items should be questioned and pointed out and the documentation returned to the applicant for full completion. A well-documented and controlled pre-employment application process is necessary for an effective and efficient hiring program.

The second step is to perform a full reference check to verify the information provided by the applicant. For whatever reason—probably legal interpretations and equal employment considerations—the amount of reference checking by employers throughout the United States has been inconsistent. Dishonest candidates have taken advantage of inconsistencies and can thwart the employment process in strange and alarming ways. This has created a problem for the candidates who would prefer to be honest in presenting themselves. However, they know that unless they also embellish who they are, they may be left behind. The whole situation has resulted in a serious and increasing mess in today's job market. Exhibit 2-1 shows specifically what job seekers may do to win a job.

CHECK THEIR EDUCATION HISTORY

In the area of education, surveys repeatedly show that a college degree greatly increases a person's earning power. Studies have also shown that with each degree earned the income-earning potential is significantly increased. When we compare the median income of college-educated workers with that of high-school-educated workers, we can see that college graduates have a higher income. Is it any wonder that someone who did not finish (or even attend) college will show a degree on his or her résumé—especially when he or she thinks it will never be checked?

Unfortunately, the majority of companies do not check degrees prior to hiring employees. This lack of diligence by employers has only fueled the problem, since job seekers realize they can succeed at fabricating their level of education. As the competition for jobs has increased, many nongraduates feel compelled to say that they have a degree to stand out in the job market.

We have seen this in our own reference-checking practice. Today, about one out of ten applicants will report a bogus degree, and among sales candidates, about one out of eight is guilty of claiming a degree not earned. Uni-

Exhibit 2-1. How and why applicants misrepresent themselves.

Educational Background
    ᛩ Degree(s) never attained—to appear well educated
    ᛩ School(s) not attended—for prestige value
    ᛩ Outside course work never started/completed—to appear industrious
    ᛩ Participation in made-up campus activities—to appear well rounded

Employment History
    ᛩ Stretch dates of employment—to cover periods of unemployment
    ᛩ Omit certain employers—to hide unsatisfactory employment record
    ᛩ List company that is out of business or has been absorbed—so checking is difficult or impossible

Salary and Job Title
    ᛩ Inflate previous salary—to create higher compensation need
    ᛩ Embellish job title—to appear more successful

Expertise and Achievements
    ᛩ Indicate supervisory/management positions not held—to reflect leadership ability
    ᛩ Embellish duties and responsibilities—to appear more experienced and successful
    ᛩ Indicate performance levels not attained—to appear more competent
    ᛩ Exaggerate results achieved (sales, profits, programs)—to appear more successful

Self-Employment
    ᛩ List self-employment or personal consulting—to cover a period of unemployment or a job that did not work out
    ᛩ Exaggerate self-employed accomplishments—to appear successful

Criminal Record
  ৎ Omit convictions—to remove any doubt regarding honesty or reliability
  ৎ Downplay past record—to divert attention from personal problems

References
  ৎ List well-known or important people—to impress employer
  ৎ Program references to say the right things—to cover misrepresentation

versity officials have warned that academic fraud has assumed epidemic proportions, especially in professions that require advanced education such as health care, law, and engineering.

We have uncovered phony degrees among candidates from executives to hourly applicants. People without a college or high school degree will blatantly indicate on their résumés and employment applications that they have a certain degree and will even go so far as to include the year of graduation.

We can recall stories from our own recent experience. In one case, an applicant indicated on his résumé that he had received a bachelor's degree from a prestigious school on the East Coast. However, when we checked with the registrar's office at the university, it was unable to locate him in its records. Obviously, he never even attended the university but thought he could get away with fabricating a degree on his résumé. In another instance, an applicant claimed she had graduated from Florida State University. Again, when we went to verify her degree, we found out that although she had attended the university, she had received a failing grade in most of her classes and was dropped for nonpayment of tuition.

Many hiring officials falsely assume that because someone spells it out on paper, the information must be true. In our opinion, this is a serious injustice to those who have actually completed their education, usually at a considerable expenditure of effort and money.

Probably one of the most outlandish claims to a college degree occurred while we were checking on a salesperson for a large chemical company. When the school where he claimed to have received a B.S. degree in chemistry was contacted, we were told that he had attended for two years, but he did not graduate. When we informed the employment manager about our findings, he felt that there must be some mistake because he was looking at a copy of the applicant's transcript, which the candidate had faxed to him. He faxed the transcript copy to our office, which we in turn sent to the registrar at the school. The registrar called and explained that the top one-third of the transcript showing the candidate's name and other information was correct; however, the bottom two-thirds were from another student's transcript, in fact, one who had graduated with very good grades. What the candidate had done was paste his name and other identifying information on the top to make it look like his transcript. It was a clever composite reproduction. Even the embossed school seal showed on the bottom of the document. Because it was faxed, the glued-together document looked like the real thing. (See Exhibit 2-2.)

You have to wonder how many executives and other key people do not have the level of credentials they claim. Although it is probably not a major problem, it is still more prevalent than we care to admit.

By not checking someone's reported degree, you are asking to be lied to. Even more important, it can lead to hiring an underqualified person or someone who will con-

Exhibit 2-2. Hot tips.

When asking an applicant to provide documentation to support his or her educational credentials, always obtain original documentation. With advances in technology, manufacturing a copy of a diploma or degree is as simple as a few easy keystrokes. It is more difficult, however, to re-create a school's educational seal, which is present on all original documents. If an applicant indicates that an original is not available, it is necessary to validate, directly with the school, the copy's authenticity.

tinue to lie as an employee. Applicants who lie about their degrees are willing to take the risk because past history shows that most employers do not take the time to verify education.

It is easy to confirm attendance and degrees at most U.S. and foreign colleges simply by calling the registrar's office of the school. Many schools are now using an outside service to record and confirm this information for a nominal fee. With few exceptions, you can verify school attendance and degrees over the telephone, and this procedure usually takes no more than four to eight minutes to complete. Try calling your own school to see how easy it is to obtain this information.

Colleges and universities should provide this service as a way of recognizing their graduates, and also to keep imposters from getting a free education from the school. A few schools will not give the information over the telephone, which we feel is a terrible mistake because word gets out and dishonest applicants will use that school as an easy mark, which is unfair to the real graduates.

High schools will normally verify graduation over the telephone or by fax. A date of birth and the year graduated are usually all the information required.

We suggest you always start your reference-checking

process by verifying the education claimed. If you find a discrepancy there, you probably will not want to proceed any further. If someone tells you that he graduated from the University of Notre Dame in South Bend, Ohio, beware.

WATCH FOR GAPS IN THEIR CAREER HISTORY

Some job candidates, in an attempt to hide the gaps in their employment history, stretch the dates during which they were actually employed. We have had candidates who had actually been incarcerated, seriously ill, or in drug rehabilitation but chose to cover up by extending dates of employment. In other cases, they simply decided to take some time off or could not find new employment. Rather than having to explain their absence from the working world, they chose to drop this time from their résumés or employment applications by falsifying the actual dates they were employed at certain places.

It is very important that an applicant explain long gaps in her employment history in detail.

THE "X" FACTOR

To see how deception and dishonesty occur in the job market, let's examine the "X" factor, shown in Exhibit 2-3. The "X" factor is simply two lines. The control line represents the amount of checking done by the employer; the reaction line is the amount of lying done by applicants. What it shows is that as the amount of checking decreases, the amount of lying increases.

Now let's look at how this phenomenon affects individual companies. If it becomes known that your company does not do background checking, you can bet that

Exhibit 2-3. The "X" factor at work.

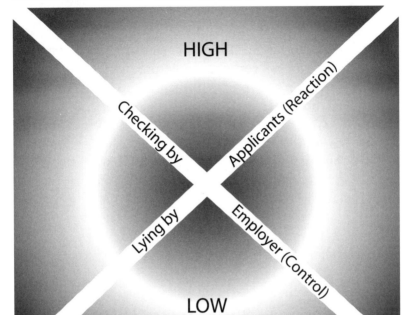

people in the job market are aware of this and are probably taking advantage of the situation.

We tell people who attend our seminars on employment screening that while they are sleeping, dishonest
applicants are thinking up ways to fool employers. We relate the story of an employee at a large manufacturing
plant who was required to do heavy lifting as part of his
job responsibilities. He had been employed with the company for about three months when he hurt his back on
the job. Upon examination by the company doctor, the
company officials were informed that he had a deformed
back and should not be working or doing heavy lifting.
The ironic part is that this same doctor had originally
given this person a pre-employment physical and had

given him a clean bill of health. After an investigation, it turned out that the employee had arranged for someone else to take his physical for him.

Needless to say, this person was released from the company and a new companywide procedure was immediately put into place that required all applicants to sign a health questionnaire in front of someone at the employment office. This was then compared with the picture and signature on their driver's license. They also had to countersign the form at the doctor's office. Using a driver's license is a good way to double-check whom you are really working with.

THE HONESTY/COMPETENCY MATRIX

When we screen job candidates, we are consciously or subconsciously trying to determine two factors. We want to find out how honest they are being with us, and we want to be able to predict how competent they will be on the job. The matrix in Exhibit 2-4 shows that some applicants see no need to be anything but completely honest. However, the vast majority of people fall into that great middle group of the average, or slightly above or below average. Therefore, among a group of candidates interviewed for a position, each person will fall somewhere along a spectrum of talents and abilities.

The majority of applicants will generally tell you what you want to hear. Every candidate would like for you to believe that he or she is the ideal person for the job opening. The person will lead you to think that he or she is being completely honest and is a top performer in his or her field. If you are interviewing someone for an accounting position and a specific type of software program is essential, chances are the candidate will quickly recall a situation, no matter how large or small his or her

Exhibit 2-4. The honesty/competency matrix.

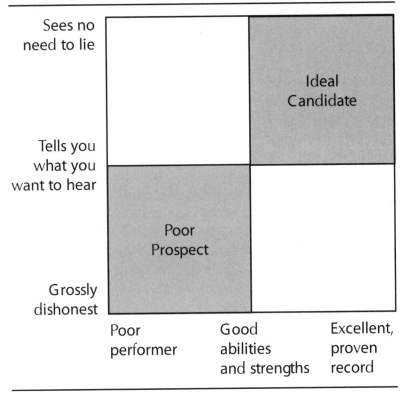

involvement was, where he or she worked with this particular program. The candidate picks up on your signals and tells you what you want to hear. This also happens in our personal lives with our children. You are concerned about the people your teenage son is associating with, so you ask, "Are those good kids you are spending your time with?" Naturally, he will pick up on your clue and reply with something he knows you want to hear, such as, "Sure, they are. Why, Steven's dad is a doctor and Katherine's dad is a minister." He took your cue and gave you the reassurance you wanted. However, if you continue to probe into the answers given, chances are you will find the truth that you are seeking.

On the honesty/competency matrix of Exhibit 2-4, a few people are proven top performers. Then there are those who are chronically poor performers, some of whom do not even realize that they are at this low level. Most people, however, generally fall into the average category of performance. No matter what the job level or category, there are top performers, average performers, and low performers. When the president of the United States leaves office, what does he worry about? He wonders whether he will go down in history as a great president, average one, or poor one.

Management's View of Employment

Executives, managers, and staff members in organizations throughout the country invariably tell us that most of the time they check the references of prospective employees who are applying for jobs with their company. Middle managers, who are closer to what is actually going on, say that the references of their job candidates get checked about 75 percent of the time. However, the staff personnel actually responsible for doing the checking will admit that references get checked in only about 50 percent of the cases, and even then, it is not always done thoroughly.

The point is that upper management knows the benefit of checking the backgrounds of those hired by the company. It is just good business sense. However, the problem is that down on the working level the whole process of checking out job applicants is shortchanged or not done at all. Often, the hiring professional does not have the time necessary to perform an accurate and thorough search of an applicant's background.

Nothing predicts a person's future job performance more accurately than previous work habits. Background

checks that include a thorough investigation of employment references will enhance the "fit" between employees and the employer's culture. Thorough background
checks are simply a good management practice.

DON'T BE FOOLED

Pyrite, a mineral that is light yellow with a metallic luster,
was often mistaken for real gold during the gold rush
years. It fooled enough prospectors to inspire its nick-
name, "fool's gold." To be certain of what they had, the
prospectors would have it assayed.

Unfortunately, job candidates who give the appearance and impression of being the real thing have similarly
fooled many interviewers. However, under close examination through background checking, they turned out to be
not so exceptional. Some applicants tell you about who
and what they would like to be rather than who and what
they really are. Do not assume that someone is even mar-
ginally competent, no matter how good he or she claims
to be. During the interview, make the candidate give you
clear examples of proven job performance. If a candidate
makes it into the final stage of the interviewing process,
this information can be confirmed when you speak with
previous supervisors. If the candidate is unable to provide
examples of good performance, then move on to the next
person.

Sometimes the desire to speed up the hiring process
can create a serious problem. A number of organizations
extend job offers contingent on successful completion of
a background check. Because of the need to fill a position,
an offer is made and many people start work before the
background check is completed. A company we are familiar with placed a candidate in a director position and then
learned she had lied about her education. She was imme-

diately dismissed for falsification of the information she supplied. However, because of the company's rush to fill the position, it lost three months of its training investment and, of course, had to recruit for the position again. The entire episode took a great deal of time—to say nothing of the disruption it caused.

Checking references should be the final step in the employment process. Go through the full evaluation process and then check the references for the person you feel is best suited for the position. You will now be able to confirm that what you have been led to believe about the person you have chosen for the job is, in fact, true. Some employers will check references on all of their final candidates to obtain information upon which to base a final selection decision. We do not necessarily recommend this as an effective way to use reference checking because it places too much emphasis on what the references have to say, and even more important, it strains the whole system because of the heavy workload it creates. Also, checking out a large number of final candidates may cause the rejected applicants to think they did not get the job based on what their references said, which may not be the case at all.

However, if you choose to select a candidate by this method, you may want to think about outsourcing the entire reference-checking process to a company specializing in background investigations. Professional background checkers can uncover a great deal of information and are able to spend the time necessary to obtain the information you need to make a sound hiring decision. A clerical or low-level employee should never check references because they are not trained in how to ask the tough questions that will provide useful information.

Checking the background of job candidates has never been more important. On the other hand, owing to reorganizations and downsizing, most companies and the people who do the employment screening have less time than ever to devote to the task. They are already overworked, and consequently this function is often neglected. We are entering a new era that requires new thinking and actions to get us back on track.

Screening Options

THERE ARE MANY SCREENING OPTIONS available to employers. Listed below are additional actions that can be taken to check out applicants. Of course, not every option should be exercised for every candidate. For example, for plant or general labor, the verification of education may not be applicable. The type of position, company policy, and the availability of the information will determine the extent of the check.

The following screening options are available:

- Employment history
- Performance ability and accomplishments
- Personality traits
- Supervisory potential and ability
- Educational background and verification
- Credit history
- Criminal records check
- Professional licenses and registrations
- Driving record
- Civil record search
- Military service record
- Social security verification

The first four factors listed are normally considered to be reference checking. The remaining options are usually referred to as background checks. Employers who want to do their own screening will find the proper techniques in this book. Some employers prefer to use a pre-employment screening company to handle parts of or the entire task. Regardless of whether the employer does the screening or it is outsourced, familiarity with the points and issues discussed in these pages will enhance the effectiveness and results obtained. In all cases, the employer should remain in full control of the screening process and the hiring decision.

ADDITIONAL SCREENING METHODS

Rather than relying solely on interviewing, reference checking, and background checks, many employers are using various other means to evaluate job candidates. The most common methods being used are outlined here.

Psychological Testing

The use of psychological testing to screen candidates is not new. These tests, ranging from paper-and-pencil exercises to in-depth psychological interviews, are designed to provide employers with more information about a candidate's personal characteristics and profile, such as honesty, intelligence, reliability, work ethic, and congeniality. The tests attempt to provide a handle on qualities and traits that may not be detectable during interviews or background screening. Testing is considered a good way to get into the "real" person. Many employers see testing as a safety net for their hiring program.

Drug Testing

Preemployment and random drug testing have been legal for many years. The employment of drug abusers is known to increase absenteeism, health care costs, and potential liability, as well as loss of productivity. There is no question that a high percentage of people have a drug problem and that drug abusers can become a drain on the organization. It is legal to perform drug testing during the employment process, if done on a stated and consistent basis.

Handwriting Analysis

Using someone's handwriting as a means by which to better understand that person is an old practice. A few employers are using handwriting analysis as a tool for screening applicants. A sample of the applicant's handwriting is reviewed by a so-called expert, who then renders an opinion on what it reveals about the person.

Skill and Aptitude Tests

There are written examinations available that test an individual's knowledge of a particular subject or the ability to learn and handle the subject. These tests can also include demonstrating one's ability to perform certain physical tasks and responsibilities. However, this is an area that can result in a discrimination charge, if not handled properly.

Lie Detector Tests

Most employers are prohibited from using lie detector tests for employment under the federal Employee Polygraph Protection Act. Only occupations that involve national or private security can consider such testing. There is considerable debate about the validity and reliability of polygraph testing.

The discussion in this section is only for information and is not meant to be complete or a recommendation for using these screening methods. It is important that professional and legal input be obtained before any major decision is made regarding employment processing.

AVOIDING THE PROBLEM ALTOGETHER

You can avoid hiring completely unknown people by being your own recruiter. There is nothing that prevents an organization from going out on its own to recruit proven, top performers whom it knows about. Most line or staff managers belong to associations or have some contact with other people in their specialty or career field. They have met or at least heard about individuals with excellent reputations. If you are looking for a state tax supervisor, for example, think of those with a top standing in this field. Call these people and let them know you have a position opening. If they are interested, have them come in or at least ask them to think about it and to call you back if they would like to pursue the opportunity.

Any employment specialist worth his salt will always ask the manager with an opening if he or she knows of anyone in particular who would fit in the job. Then you can start your search with these candidates. If you turn an opening over to an outside recruiting company, it will often ask whether there are any individuals you would like to interview. It will then contact those persons and, if possible, feed them back to you. Why not avoid the expense and do it yourself? If it bothers you to make this contact as a representative of your company, hire someone to do it at a fraction of what you would have to pay to have these people eventually sent to you as a result of an expensive outside search effort.

Because of the difficulty in trying to screen job candidates today, a rapidly growing trend among organizations is to use temporary employees who can be cut loose if they are not suitable or are not working out well on the job. A company can then hire permanent employees from this pool of people, after observing them over a period of time. The temp-to-hire program allows you to evaluate candidates on a trial basis before hiring them. However, there is a downside to using these people. The cost per hour for their services can be much higher than what you would pay if they were on your payroll.

If you are looking for a job and hear that a certain company that you would like to work for has an opening, contact that company and let the people there know of your interest before they have to start an expensive and time-consuming recruiting effort. You may find that you have practically clear sailing into the job. Send them a list of ten ways in which you can help the company meet its goals. Why wait for the opening to appear in the newspaper, when you then become just one of the many unknown respondents with which a company must deal?

The experience of most employers is that the best candidates come through referrals from employees, customers, professional networks, trade organizations, and even schools and churches. Use all the resources available to you. The practice of paying employees a fee for referrals who are hired and stay for three months, six months, or a year is often a bargain in the recruiting process.

A little initiative by both the employer and the candidate can go a long way toward solving the dilemma of the unknown applicant who must be carefully screened and checked out to avoid unexpected future surprises after he or she starts work.

The Candidate's Advantage

JOB SEEKERS HAVE INNUMERABLE SERVICES, specialists, and products available to improve their interviewing skills. There is an entire industry devoted to helping candidates, including career counseling or outplacement assistance, professional résumé writers, search firms, and employment agencies, to say nothing of the numerous books, audiocassettes, and videotapes on how to find a job, and even computer programs to track the entire job search. Let's look more closely at each of these and see how they can help and, in many cases, add polish to an applicant.

CAREER COUNSELING AND OUTPLACEMENT

Most of us probably went to career counselors in high school or college. Counselors are often teachers who may not really know or be experienced in the business world. If reasonably competent, however, counselors can help to point job seekers in the right direction.

Outplacement comes in two forms: retail and company paid. You have probably seen advertisements for retail career-planning (or management or development or transition) firms in big-city newspapers and telephone books. These firms cater to those who are looking for jobs or want to make a career change. They try to find candidates who are finding their search too time-consuming or unproductive—and charge a substantial fee to help them. They emphasize their career-marketing services for moving candidates through the job market by using planning and personal assistance programs.

Corporations attempting to help terminated employees obtain new jobs often retain company-paid outplacement firms. They start out by trying to minimize the trauma associated with termination and then develop a structured program to guide employees in their job search. They usually prepare résumés and give personalized attention to each individual with follow-up guidance as needed. Their goal is to reduce the time needed to locate a new position. Their fees, which vary depending on the level of service provided, are based on a prearranged understanding and are usually paid for by the candidate's last employer.

Both retail and company-paid services follow a similar outline that involves explaining the realities of the job market, writing an effective résumé, developing techniques to generate interviews, targeting industries and organizations, and helping with letter-writing campaigns. Many also provide interview training with actual practice on videotape. Obviously, a good firm can be a tremendous help to job candidates in understanding and tackling the tough chore of finding the right new job.

RÉSUMÉ-PREPARATION SERVICES

At one time, a résumé indicated a candidate's writing ability and knowledge of grammar. That is no longer true.

The higher the job level sought by a candidate, the greater the chance that the résumé was prepared professionally. Résumé-writing services, both formal and informal, now abound everywhere. A high percentage of résumés are either entirely written or at least rewritten for job hunters. At the executive level, almost all résumés have a professional touch.

A résumé basically says: Here is where I have worked, what I did, and how good I was. Experts in the employment field advise that the primary purpose of a résumé is to get the initial interview. After all, a résumé is examined for only about twenty seconds before a decision is made whether or not to consider the candidate. It is in the interview that the candidate must sell himself or herself to get a job. The résumé should therefore be succinct and to the point—like a good product advertisement. It should contain just enough information to convince the employer to call the person in for an interview. Unfortunately, many candidates create long and rambling documents that are actually boring and self-defeating. A candidate is ahead of the competition if the résumé does nothing to unsell his or her candidacy.

You might ask, so what if a résumé is puffed up a little bit? Perhaps you believe that all attempts should be used in the résumé to present the candidate in the best light. The problem is that the résumé is the candidate's script and, if it is exaggerated or falsified, that message has to be carried out through the entire hiring process by the candidate.

JOB-HUNTING BOOKS, TAPES, AND COMPUTER PROGRAMS

There are many books, audiotapes, and videotapes on the market that explain how to succeed in the job search and find new employment. Most of them are good and offer sound advice to the perplexed, confused, or even desperate job seeker. Looking for a job is a rough situation for most people and even quite frightening for many. Therefore, any help or encouragement they can get is desirable and needed.

There is a growing emphasis on the use of computers and online databases that match job seekers to positions and recruiters to job seekers, or allow an individual to scan openings that may be of interest. There are a variety of computerized databases that give applicants the opportunity to research companies or industries quickly and comprehensively according to their size, revenues, product, location, or any other meaningful combination. Such comprehensive resources provide ready information to job seekers and reduce the amount of time ordinarily spent on researching target companies and trying to figure out what they want. Through database resource companies, it is now possible to pinpoint the person to whom you should send your résumé. Thus, more time and attention can be spent on actually trying to capture the position sought, which further tips the whole process toward the applicant.

SEARCH FIRMS AND EMPLOYMENT AGENCIES

Talking about the advantages candidates have in the job market would not be complete without mentioning the way search firms and employment agencies go out of their way to help candidates. Let's face it, search firms and agencies have one purpose—to place people in new jobs and to be paid for it. Although these services may extol their desire to match the right people with the right job, the bottom line is that they have to place people somewhere in order to pay their bills and stay in business.

The first step these firms take is to identify their candidate's strong points and then sell prospective employers on interviewing this candidate. The agency usually does a better job than a job hunter would have done on the candidate's behalf, because most people are not comfortable bragging about themselves. They will then prepare the person for the interview by telling him or her what the company, the job, and the interviews are like. They will often go into great detail on what questions to anticipate and how to answer them. They may even advise the candidate on the idiosyncrasies and preferences of the company's interviewers, so that the candidate will be better prepared to handle or even to take control of the interview. An employment consultant may spend up to two hours coaching a candidate on how to beat the interview and win the job.

We have seen written summaries from employment firms that were really "cooked"; that is, they omitted important and unfavorable items of information, or cleverly disguised negative points so that they did not appear to be the problems they actually were. In fact, we have seen summaries in which dates of employment had been moved around to make a candidate's employment record look as if he had been continuously employed during his career. However, after performing a full background check on this individual, several gaps in employment were found. We have also seen cases where a degree is listed and the candidate either never received a degree or in some cases never even attended the university.

APPEARANCES MAY BE MISLEADING

The candidate who stands before an interviewer is at his or her very best. He or she probably has on a new suit or dress, has spruced up for the occasion, and is making a real effort to be a pleasant and likable human being. We have all had to look for a job and know that we have to put our best foot forward to make a good impression. Someone who smokes, for example, knows not to light up a cigarette during an interview, even though he is an inveterate smoker who normally cannot go fifteen minutes without smoking.

The following story was told in the first edition of this book, but we feel it needs repeating because it clearly shows how we can be completely fooled during the hiring process:

A client told us about a receptionist she had hired. The company is an elite firm and is housed in a beautiful building with modern and impressive offices. It wanted this image quickly projected to its visitors. The manager twice interviewed a young woman who seemed to have it all. She was pretty, well dressed, and well spoken. She seemed like a perfect fit for the receptionist position. However, when she came to work the first day, staff members could hardly believe their eyes. Her hair and makeup were almost outlandish, her clothes were trendy, and her speech and actions were completely different from what she had projected in the interview.

To make a long story short, she had borrowed both outfits she wore when being interviewed; a friend had helped her with her hair and makeup so that she would project a more businesslike image; and she even had coaching on how to speak and act in a more mature manner. She had portrayed the role very well and got the job, but in fact, she was a very young girl who did not have a business wardrobe and really did not want to conform to the style of a professional environment. Her initial appearance was a façade. She was immediately released from the company and it had to start its search over again.

This happens every day. It is the way the game is played. Men are told to shave off their beards if they have one, get a haircut, wear a conservative suit, shine their shoes, cover up tattoos, etc. Women are told to adopt a businesslike appearance and demeanor, to wear only the most conservative jewelry, and are given other pertinent advice suitable to the level and type of position for which they are applying.

The most common pitfall recruiters face is to be dazzled by personality. Even top recruiters may confuse an applicant's interview skills with the skills he or she will need on the job. We are all vulnerable to charmers.

We have heard numerous applicants for hourly plant work brag about their good work habits and steady attendance. After being hired, usually without a background check, they start doing poor work and come in late or are often absent. How many times have we heard stories about employees who have helped take care of their sick or dying grandparents? Isn't it amazing how many employees have a sick relative? Maybe reference checking should include finding out the number and health of an applicant's grandparents.

Anyone who has done a lot of hiring can relate similar stories of candidates who shine during the interview and then, when hired, display poor work habits or a bad attitude. After all, an employer would not knowingly hire someone who was not going to work out in the job. Applicants know this and, almost by reflex, paint a glowing picture of themselves to get the job.

Ultimately, what you see and hear when you interview someone is not always what you get in the end. The hiring situation often becomes a big game of fooling the interviewer. Fortunately, you can find out what the person is really like if you take the time and effort to go back and talk with the people who have known or worked with the applicant in the past. The information is there—if you take the time to seek it out.

INFLATED SALARIES

Many job candidates overstate their compensation to some extent. Salary deception has become epidemic because individuals believe it is one way to get ahead. Moreover, it is relatively easy for job seekers to lie because few businesses bother to verify past salaries. Employers do not want to offend job candidates. They are more concerned with getting the right person than with whether they are offering too much.

Pay deception is a problem employers have to deal with every day. Many job candidates believe that dishonesty does pay. Some applicants fudge their pay simply because they think it is standard procedure. People in the job market ask each other: "How much are you going to tell them you make?" It has become part of the cat-and-mouse game that goes on during the interview process.

Unfortunately, too many companies rely primarily on a candidate's current pay, or what they think it is, rather than on the job level itself. That is fine if it is on the high side. But if a person is underpaid, that situation tends to be perpetuated in the next job, since companies unfairly take advantage of the low starting point. This is largely why women and minorities are often paid less than their white male counterparts.

More companies are starting to check applicants' pay history. Some verify salary levels by demanding W-2 income forms from job seekers. But even well-crafted plans are not foolproof. Many job candidates refuse to produce W-2 forms. And, let's face it, there are ways to come up with a fake W-2 form. Again, the employer must always be on guard and be able to decipher the truth versus the nontruth.

Part I Summary

In Part I you found that:

- The growing problem of dishonesty by job applicants has become a major business concern.
- Job applicants often lie or falsify information so that they appear to be the best candidate for the position.
- By not checking out what an applicant tells you, many questionable individuals will take advantage of the situation and gain access to jobs they are not qualified to hold.
- Eventually, even honest people will resort to falsification to keep up with the dishonest ones who are getting by on false pretenses.
- Because of increasing dishonesty in the job market today, now more than ever, companies need to be diligent and thoroughly check what they are being told by job applicants.

The Legalities and Confusion Surrounding Employment

The Real Problem in Employment

WE BELIEVE THAT LAWYERS HAVE effectively crippled the nation's hiring efforts and encouraged lying, cover-ups, and failure by telling companies not to talk with each other about past employees.

There are several reasons why we make these claims:

ᕯ *Lying.* Knowing that their work history probably will not be checked, many candidates lie and get away with it, which is causing even honest applicants to cheat to stay in the running.

ᕯ *Cover-ups.* Protecting poor performers, which penalizes those with good records, is hardly a fair way to reward good service. In today's world, many companies are downsizing because of economic conditions, so it only makes sense to help laid-off workers become gainfully employed as soon as possible. By not speaking about someone, it will appear to a future employer that he may not have been a good employee, which ultimately costs him the job.

ק *Failure.* Being told to check out the people you hire
when everyone else has been told not to provide such information means you are literally setting yourself up to
fail. Most hiring officials admit that they will not exchange information with each other because their attorneys have instructed them not to.

THE LAWYERS' PERSPECTIVE

When giving advice on what to tell someone who contacts
a former employer or supervisor about a past employee,
attorneys advise providing only name, rank, and serial
number. In other words, provide only dates of employment and job title, and perhaps verify salary level if the
caller already knows it.

Attorneys advise against providing information on
whether the candidate is eligible for rehire or the reason
for separation. They say that it is dangerous to say anything about a past employee because doing so could lead
to a lawsuit.

Conversely, attorneys will also tell you to get all the
information you can about a prospective employee, because employer liability for bad hiring decisions is on the
rise. This amounts to legal doublespeak. Do not tell anyone anything about a former employee when contacted,
but expect companies to tell you everything when you
contact them.

The courts are now holding companies legally responsible for the actions of their employees and holding
them responsible for bad hiring decisions. This basically
means that employers should have known or should have
put forth more effort in trying to learn more about the
person they hired. Damage awards in such cases can be
substantial.

In our reference-checking business, we have been

amazed at how often client companies ask us to get all the background data and information about a prospective employee that we can find. Yet, when we contact these same companies to get information for another client, they tell us that company policy prohibits them from giving any information to anyone. Everyone from top to bottom seems to be thoroughly confused on this critical legal issue.

LET'S CORRECT THE PROBLEM

There are two sides to reference checking: getting and giving references. The policy of only giving the basic information about a former employee evolved over the past several decades as an easy way to avoid lawsuits for defamation, which could result if someone provided a negative reference.

This type of a company policy does not make good management sense. Companies that do not give reference information will not get information in return. Withholding information about the work habits of former employees prevents prospective employers from making informed hiring decisions based on real facts.

The whole game has become confusing to everyone, especially those in charge of getting or giving out information on employees. They have been told that their company can be held liable for disclosing too much information or too little information, or for failing to not get enough information about a candidate whom they hire. Hiring professionals are confused and upset over this conflicting legal advice.

Unfortunately, the traditional legal advice of getting all the information you can without giving any out has helped to create the current problems in employment law. This is not only poor legal advice but also terrible management advice. It has led to paranoia in the hiring process and lying on applications and résumés. Everyone is confused on the subject, and even the attorneys are fighting among themselves.

Some attorneys who work in this field, however, have been offering a different approach. They are questioning the wisdom of advice that allows bad employees to pass from employer to employer and punishes good employees who deserve the benefit of a positive referral.

In actual practice, many employers give and receive references all the time, simply because this information is necessary to employ a quality workforce. The best course of action is to check references, to provide references, and to do so correctly.

Does your company have a policy stating that any action taken against an employee must be documented and signed by the employee? Does your company perform yearly or periodic performance reviews? With documented evidence of poor performance or problems on the job, a person does not have a leg to stand on if he feels negative information was given about him. If you had an employee with an attendance problem and the times he was late or absent are documented, then how can someone argue that he did not have a problem? If your company does not adequately keep their employee records up-to-date and document employee actions, then we can see why you may be reluctant to provide information.

WHY CHECK AN APPLICANT'S BACKGROUND?

Let's look at why it is important to know as much as possible about the people you hire. Many hiring managers are unaware of the extent to which their organizations are accountable for their employees' actions. Employers have been found liable for theft, sexual assault, robbery, and wrongful death because of an employee's misconduct.

The employer can be held liable for an employee's unlawful acts when the employer does not reasonably investigate a potential employee's background and puts the employee in a position to commit crimes or exposes others to the risk of harm or injury from that employee.

As a rule, employers may be found liable if:

- ๔ The injury or harm is foreseeable.
- ๔ Hiring or retaining the employee puts him or her in a position to commit the act, even though the act is beyond his or her job responsibilities.
- ๔ The employer knew or should have known, based on a reasonable investigation, that the employee was not suitable for the duties of the position.

With negligent-hiring lawsuits being brought in nearly all jurisdictions, prehiring practices such as thorough reference checking should become a key part of any employer's preventive law program.

The federal government and many states have laws requiring applicants in certain fields to undergo a background check before they are hired. Many states, for example, require background checks before qualifying attorneys, private investigators, law enforcement officials, and child-care providers.

So how much screening is enough to avoid liability? The amount of screening must be proportionate to the degree of risk presented by the job to be filled. The focus must be on the position to be filled, not on the applicant.

DOES IT REALLY HAPPEN?

Here are some actual stories of people who were not what their employers thought they would be:

In a recent New York State negligent-hiring case, a supermarket in Westchester County was ordered to pay half of a $1.15 million damage award to a former employee who had been stabbed by a coworker in the store's parking lot. The knife-wielding employee, it was subsequently learned, had a record of violent criminal behavior in another state. Although the supermarket did not know of the assailant's criminal past when it hired him, the court ruled that it should have known or found out about his past before hiring him.

A plumbing company sent one of its employees to do work at a jewelry store. While he was performing the work, he stole some jewelry. The owner sued the plumbing company when it was discovered that the employee had a long criminal history of theft. The court found the plumbing company guilty of negligent hiring, stating that a proper background check was not performed prior to hiring, which would have uncovered his past history.

A security company hired an individual as a security guard and did not conduct a criminal records check on him. Shortly after he was employed, he struck and seriously injured a woman in the building he was guarding because she questioned his authority. A court found this security company liable because it was felt that it was the company's responsibility to check into the guard's background prior to putting him on the job. The court went on to say that a reasonably adequate investigation would have determined that the guard was unfit for the job.

AUTHORIZATION AND RELEASE

Under the Fair Credit Reporting Act, employers must include in their job application process a separate and conspicuous document that states that: (1) a background check may be performed on every person the company is considering hiring, and (2) the applicant authorizes such a check and releases the company from all liability for performing the investigation. By signing this authorization, the applicant acknowledges that he or she has read the release and consents to a background check that will include reference checks with prior employers, and may also cover education, criminal, workers compensation, credit, and driving records. At times, an applicant may refuse to sign this form, or simply get up and leave because of his or her past history. For further discussion on this matter, see Chapter 8 and Exhibit 8-2.

THE COST OF RUNNING SCARED

A certain amount of legal expense should be considered as part of the normal cost of doing business. Ironically, many companies today are spending more to prevent lawsuits related to employment practices than it would cost them to defend against such suits if they were brought. Actually, the direct cost of defending oneself in such lawsuits is normally quite small because few actions result in suits. The threat of litigation, more than the actual lawsuits themselves, is causing companies to behave in ways that drive up hiring costs and also affect their ability to hire.

One of the possible hidden costs to companies is the expense of hiring poor performers rather than passing over them. The cost of checking a person's background is far less than the money that will be spent in training and benefits for a person that does not work out after a few months.

In addition, some companies, as part of their defensive strategy, may be providing more overtime pay to a reduced workforce or using easy-to-terminate but expensive temporary workers instead of hiring full-time employees. These indirect costs can exceed the cost of defending the company against legal actions.

Companies are behaving as if the odds of being sued are much higher than they actually are. Whereas employers once felt they had considerable leeway in choosing their employees, they have now gone too far in the other direction. There is no question that legal and regulatory considerations cannot be ignored, but interpretations of employment law in each state have been both broad and narrow, and vary greatly from state to state and even from case to case.

The legal picture is somewhat different in the employment setting. First, it is difficult for applicants to determine why they were turned down for a job unless you choose to tell them. Second, the burden of proving that statements made by a company representative about a past or current employee were false or that they were made carelessly, recklessly, or maliciously are difficult burdens for the plaintiff to meet.

According to a survey conducted by the Society for Human Resource Management (SHRM), few employers have experienced legal difficulties resulting from references provided to other employers regarding prospective employees. Only 1 percent of respondents said that defamation claims have been brought against their organizations as a result of references provided about former employees. In our many years in the employment field, we can only recall a half dozen instances where candidates have challenged what a previous employer said about them. And, all of these fell by the wayside and were not pursued to a legal conclusion. It is the fear of being sued rather than the experience of being sued that prompts the tight limitations companies place on providing information about current or past employees.

Indeed, a running-scared attitude is probably the least effective (and most costly) way to handle employment problems. The strategies and techniques suggested in this book are safer and less expensive than the defensive actions you may be taking. Simply reducing your legal exposure is not necessarily the best way to go about hiring the workforce you need. We believe attorneys rate a D minus for the way they have guided the U.S. employment scene. It is our hope that this book will help to straighten out the mess they have created.

Who Is Actually Running Human Resources?

THE DECISION TO RELEASE INFORMATION should be based on sound business and commonsense considerations. Human resources (HR) professionals need to be willing to make these decisions rather than simply cite company policy in the erroneous belief that they are minimizing their company's risk.

When a proposed course of action is legal and in compliance with applicable regulations, why delay or question its implementation? There is no doubt that companies need guidance on ways to handle complex HR issues. But the practice of playing it safe and relying on legal counsel on almost a daily basis raises a legitimate question about HR's value to the organization.

THE LAW AND GOOD BUSINESS

The law is on the side of employers. Employers have a right to discuss their employees with others who have a common interest in them. It is a fundamental legal principle that neither true statements nor statements of opinion can be defamatory, no matter how hurtful they are. Employers are liable for defamation only when they knowingly or recklessly spread false information.

The majority of states have enacted good faith laws that shield employers from civil liability when giving references, and this number is expected to keep growing. This means a previous employer should not be held liable for giving a reference about date and duration of employment, pay level, job description/duties, wage history, the reason for separation from the company, and whether it was voluntary or involuntary.

In the states that have passed legislation, however, many employers are still reluctant to use the laws. Often, it has to do with corporate policies. Some employers do not appear to trust the law and are not willing to change their corporate policies. They seem confused as to how they can use the law to improve their hiring process.

We suggest you check to see whether you are in a state that has passed new reference-checking laws. A qualified local attorney can certainly provide guidance.

A NEW DIRECTION

The increase in workplace violence and negligent hiring lawsuits provides good business and legal justification for employers to perform background checks on all potential employees. As discussed in Chapter 5, performing a background check on a job applicant minimizes the employer's exposure to a negligent hiring lawsuit if the employee later harms a customer or another employee.

Clearly, pre-employment screening is a business necessity in today's environment. Employment screening should involve a careful assessment of the prospective employee's résumé or application as well as contact with previous employers and personal references.

In some situations, an employer is well advised to research an applicant's past criminal record. Such a search is not necessary in all cases, as long as the employer makes an adequate inquiry into the prospective employee's general and job-specific fitness. A criminal record search is particularly appropriate when an applicant's position involves safety, protection of property, or any risk of harm to coworkers or customers.

Before hiring anyone, most attorneys emphasize the following points:

¶ Learn as much as you can about a person before extending a job offer.
¶ Do not hire if you are uncertain about a candidate's past activities and accomplishments.

Now more than ever, employers have the opportunity to obtain and explore detailed information regarding prospective employees and to provide detailed references on former employees without fear of reprisal. The decision to do one or both should be based on all the factors that influence any normal business decision, such as whether an effort is worth the expected return.

This open exchange of information can only lead to a better workforce among employers who use the law to their advantage. It is time for companies to get rid of old ideas and start exercising their right to check out job candidates thoroughly.

GETTING AND GIVING REFERENCES

Information about job candidates is exchanged informally all the time. Friends talk to friends; employees of one company talk to employees of another company; managers talk to other managers in their specialty; and certainly executives talk to other executives and even sit on the same boards of directors with them. Job seekers often list current members of a company as personal references, which means that they want these people to talk freely with potential employers. The point is simply that job-related information is continually exchanged in the everyday world—regardless of what attorneys may advise.

More attorneys are now advising employers to release information with caution. Many companies are now updating their reference-checking policies and procedures to make them more realistic and practical. We would like to note that we have never had an attorney we contacted—as a reference for a person he or she knew—who did not fully cooperate with us and provide complete information about the applicant.

We know of an employer who will, as a matter of policy, actually read over the telephone the last performance review of a former employee. We think this is a stroke of genius, because it means that a performance evaluation, which determines an employee's future in the company, now has an important bearing when the person is making a job change. Knowing this, a person would be foolish to let his performance slip because a poor performance record will be made known to anyone with a legitimate need for obtaining this information. Not giving out past performance information only encourages mediocrity in that it removes a major incentive for trying to maintain a good work record.

A large number of employers, as a matter of practice, give a copy of the performance review to the employee being rated. When you are hiring, why not ask to see the applicant's last two or three performance reviews? Or, if contacted for information about a past employee and your company does not allow reference information to be given, why not suggest that the prospective employer ask to see the candidate's copy of past performance reviews given by your company? This is information that is already developed and does not put a reference on the spot about the candidate. Of course, to do this, you need to be confident that your company has strong and consistent performance evaluation procedures that you are willing to stand behind.

Another suggestion in regard to giving reference information is to have, as part of the separation process, a form that terminated employees can sign to indicate whether they want reference data to be given out after they leave the company. If they allow their employment record to be discussed, do it. If they do not, explain that fact to the prospective employer and suggest that the employer review the matter with the candidate to determine why he or she did not authorize such information to be exchanged. Exhibit 6-1 is a sample Approval to Release Employment Information form.

NEGLIGENT HIRING

Negligent-hiring claims have proliferated over the last several years and often arise when an employee causes violence in the workplace. Like product liability claims—which argue that, by virtue of having a product on the market, a manufacturer is responsible for harm to the public arising from the use of that product—negligent-hiring claims argue that, by virtue of having someone on the payroll, an employer is responsible for harm to others caused by that employee.

It has now become the employer's responsibility to gather information about a potential employee. If the employer chooses to hire an individual without checking his or her background, then the employer must be willing to

Exhibit 6-1. Approval to Release Employment Information form.

When the human resources department receives a request from a prospective employer for information about a former employee, we furnish only limited information concerning:

(a) dates of employment;
(b) last job title or classification, and last applicable wage rate/salary.

We do not discuss orally, or in writing, the individual's work performance, reason for leaving, or any other information that we consider to be confidential. This confidential information is divulged only when the past employee has specifically directed us to do so.

Therefore, we would be willing to furnish such additional information if you sign the form below and return it to us. If you do not want to do this, we will advise the prospective employer that, although we can provide such information, you have not authorized us to do so. In either event, this form must be signed and sent to:

Human Resources Manager
ABC Company
1115 Any Street
Anytown, OH 12345

Print your name here: _____
(Sign one space below)

I hereby authorize ABC Company to release confidential information concerning my employment record to prospective employers upon their legitimate request for same. I acknowledge that some information divulged may be negative or positive with respect to my performance and agree that I release ABC Company, its agents, and employees from any and all liability for furnishing such information upon proper request.

_____   _____
(Signature)   (Date)

I do not authorize ABC Company to reveal information about my past employment record to anyone, including a prospective employer.

_____   _____
(Signature)   (Date)

accept the risk that if something goes wrong after that person has started working for the company, it may be held responsible.

As we explain to companies we advise on employment screening, negligent hiring is a consideration, although, frankly, we have run across very few individuals or organizations that got into legal difficulty for something they did (or did not do) during the hiring process. However, there may be criticism if a new employee does not work out as expected. Someone within the company initially hired this person, meaning that someone or a number of people did not do their jobs well.

NEGLIGENT REFERENCES

A new potential for liability is that courts may be willing to hold employers liable for negligent references. In other words, a previous employer may know that someone has traits that make him or her an undesirable employee but fails to disclose this information to a prospective employer.

Although each situation has its own set of circumstances, companies can no longer assume that they are safe as long as they say nothing. Failure to state why an employee was dismissed, even if defamatory, may carry as much risk as candidly stating the facts. Many employers have adopted the most conservative position possible, limiting the information they provide to employees' job titles and dates of employment. In doing so, they prevent other employers from gathering vital information about employees' job histories and work performance—key data in making hiring decisions, data they themselves seek when hiring their own employees.

We know a production manager who lets his employees know up front that if he is ever contacted about them after they leave the company, he will not hesitate to let a future employer know whether someone was good or bad on the job. After someone gives notice that he or she is leaving, the manager makes sure to remind the person not to let him down or "dog it" just because he or she is leaving the company. And, as far as we can tell, it has been an effective motivational tool for him. Some people might question the legality and fairness of this technique, but what could be fairer to everyone concerned than good old-fashioned truthfulness?

Nondisclosure policies can cause more lawsuits than they prevent. Defamation and invasion of privacy claims may be avoided, but negligent hiring and retention suits will replace them. Employers should reexamine their policies as to the release of employee information and take advantage of the qualified privilege doctrine that permits them to release information without fear of being sued, if they do it properly.

SIMPLIFIED GUIDELINES

In most states, companies have a legal right—and some courts say even a moral obligation—to provide prospective employers with an honest and candid appraisal of former employees. The law is summarized in Exhibit 6-2.

Exhibit 6-2. Reference information.

To stay within the law, be sure that reference information is:

1. Given in good faith
2. Factual, accurate, and job related
3. Supported by personal experience or by written documentation
4. Not motivated by personal animosity

When a prospective employer is seeking information needed to make an informed and rational hiring decision, and the former employer relates the former employee's work history in a factual manner without making statements that are known falsehoods, then the law protects the communication from a successful legal action by the former employee. If an employer stays within the boundaries of qualified privilege, a fear of lawsuits is not justified under current law.

When answering requests for job references, you and your staff do not need to clam up. Instead, you can cooperate and, at the same time, protect yourself in two ways. First, tell the truth. Provide an honest, specific evaluation of a former employee's work and abilities. Second, communicate only with someone who has a need to know. In legal lingo, most states allow an employer, who is acting in good faith, a so-called qualified privilege to say things that would otherwise be considered defamatory, as long as this information is related to the person's performance on the job. But you can lose this protection by providing more information than a prospective employer needs to satisfy its legitimate business interests or by communicating information to people who do not have a need for this information.

You will also lose the privilege's protection if a former employee can prove that you acted maliciously and intended harm or that you recklessly provided false or inaccurate information. Exhibits 6-3 and 6-4 cover legal interpretations and the basic rules to follow when giving references. They provide a condensed view of the entire legal issue. Exhibit 6-5 contains an overview of the many legal issues involved in employment and how they apply to employers. This information is general in nature; it does not take into account specific state laws or regulations and is not meant to replace the advice of a qualified attorney in the area of employment law.

Exhibit 6-3. What to say when asked about an ex-employee.

Former employees have successfully sued for slander (if their reputation was damaged by something you said), libel (if their reputation was damaged by something you wrote), or invasion of privacy (if you disclosed information that should have been kept secret).

The courts recognize that you and the prospective employer do have a "common interest" in discussing the attributes of an employee (the legal term is *qualified privilege*). You're on solid ground as long as you can back up everything you say. Trouble starts when you unload your personal feelings about the person or his or her performance. At this point, you may open yourself up for liability.

Here are three basic rules and examples to help you the next time you get a call as a reference for someone you released:

1. *Always stick to the facts.* It is acceptable to state: "Joe had an accident while operating a company vehicle." But adding that he may have been drinking could cause a legal problem and lawsuit.

2. *Do not try to harm his or her reputation.* "There were serious documented problems with Mary's work" is an acceptable critique of her poor performance. To say that she apparently had a learning disability would be asking for trouble.

3. *Do not provide an explanation to other employees about the reason someone left the company.* Even though the facts may be true, the employer is held liable for the disclosure simply because this is private information. It is always wise to keep the discussion about a departed employee to a minimum.

Exhibit 6-4. Giving references legally.

Most courts' rulings on reference checking have said that a former employer can give out information on a past employee that is pertinent to making a hiring decision, so long as the information is true or reasonably believed to be so. Basically, the courts in all states have held that employers, both former and prospective, have a "qualified privilege" to discuss an employee's past performance. When the information is given to someone with a clear need to receive it, discussion of an employee's past performance, good or bad, is permissible by law.

The law favors the release of background information among employers. This privilege is founded on a policy of promoting reliable business judgments in hiring, based on all the knowledge available in the business community. Thus, when a company releases background information that enables a potential employer to make a better hiring decision, as long as the statements are true, there is no liability for libel or slander because such statements were made in furtherance of this important social policy.

To comply with equal employment opportunity considerations and rulings, all questions asked and answers given must be job related, indicative of the individual's ability to perform the job and of his or her personality characteristics as they relate to how that person gets along with others in the work setting.

Legal Guidelines

Procedure:

1. *Policy*—Provide the same type of information for employees at all levels.
2. *Legitimate*—Communicate only with someone who has a need to know the information, normally a personnel officer or the supervisor to whom the employees will report on the new job.
3. *Document*—Keep a written log of the date information was communicated and the person spoken with.
4. *Consent*—The new employer must have written consent from the job candidate to contact references, normally part of signing off the employment application.

Information:

5. *Truthful*—The information given must be true to the best of your knowledge and there must be no intent to ruin the person's reputation. It is best if your facts can be supported by proper documentation.
6. *Job related*—Limit the information you provide to only job-related data.
7. *Not malicious*—Never give unnecessary and malicious information just to provide a better understanding of the past employee (or to harm the individual).
8. *Do not volunteer*—Answer only the actual inquiry without giving an opinion or making a conjecture.

(To win a lawsuit, the candidate would have to prove that items 5 through 8 were violated and that there was resulting damage and financial loss.)

Exhibit 6-5. Legal overview.

Fair Credit Reporting Act (FCRA)

Applies to all employers, screening firms, credit-reporting agencies, and any entity providing consumer reports. The purpose of the act is to protect consumers by defining privacy policy and regulatory agencies that provide consumer data and information. Administered by the Federal Trade Commission.

Immigration Reform & Control Act of 1986 (IRCA)

Applies to all employers and employees. Prohibits employers from hiring illegal aliens. Employers are required to verify that anyone hired after November 6, 1986, is legally entitled to work in this country. Employees must provide employers with documents that show identity and eligibility to work. Employers must complete Form I-9 attesting that each employee is a U.S. national or an alien authorized to work in this country. Administered by the U.S. Immigration and Naturalization Service.

Title VII, Civil Rights Act of 1964 as amended by Equal Employment Opportunity Act of 1972

Applies to all employers of fifteen or more people, state and local governments, public and private schools, and labor unions. Prohibits discrimination on the basis of race, color, religion, sex, or national origin. It also prohibits adverse impact practices, as well as intentional unequal treatment. Administered by the U.S. Equal Opportunity Commission.

Age Discrimination in Employment Act of 1967 and 1975

Affects employers of twenty or more people. Prohibits discrimination on the basis of age of all persons forty or older.

(continues)

Exhibit 6-5. (*continued*)

Many states also have age laws that may virtually cover every-one at all ages. Administered by the U.S. Equal Employment Opportunity Commission.

Americans with Disabilities Act (ADA)

Affects employers with fifteen or more employees. Prohibits using job applications that include questions about health or about the nature or severity of a disability. Also preemploy-ment physical examinations may not be given before a job offer is made. After an offer has been made and before the applicant begins work, an employer may require a medical exam and condition employment on the results. Adminis-tered by the U.S. Equal Employment Opportunity Commis-sion.

Legal and Illegal Questions

HIRING PROFESSIONALS BASICALLY LOOK AT the legal issues surrounding hiring in two different ways: The first group
clearly wants to check the applicant's background to ensure that candidates it hires have the skills and qualifications necessary to be successful in the organization, and
it wants to be certain it is doing it legally. The second
group wants to learn and be conversant with the legal
reasons why it is not advisable to check people's backgrounds, because the group really does not want to do it.
This group becomes part of the problem, instead of part
of the solution.

Many hours and dollars have been spent trying to
train hiring officials as to what questions they can legally
ask job applicants and their references. We have found
that this training is usually presented in a legalistic and
complicated manner that ends up confusing those doing
the hiring. In the end, it only makes them more fright-
ened and less effective at checking out job candidates.

There are two basic rules that will keep you out of
trouble 99.44 percent of the time.

1. Use the same questions with every individual applying for the position. Do not use different questions for different groups (women, minority members, and the handicapped).
2. Ask only job-related questions. Do not ask for personal information. Play it safe. Stay with questions that have to do with education, training, work history, and job-related skills.

PREVENTING EMPLOYMENT DISCRIMINATION

There was a time, not long ago, when white males primarily filled the so-called best jobs. Then, as a result of long overdue governmental and societal pressures, employers were forced to interview and consider women and minority group members for all job openings. Federal and state governments passed laws and regulations to end discrimination in employment and to ensure that everyone would be treated equally and fairly when seeking jobs.

There is a fundamental concept in employment that must be honored. The nature of the questions you ask cannot reduce the chances of being hired for minorities, women, or other specified groups. In a court of law, you must be able to show that the responses to any questions asked are not used to eliminate any member of a protected class from consideration. In other words, if the answer you get becomes a factor in your decision, and it would eliminate a member of any single group, you must ensure it does not get into a possible discrimination area. Even if the candidate introduces the topic, you should avoid asking about or discussing anything that involves a person's sex, race, color, religion, national origin, age, or physical disability.

We all know that we figuratively must jump hurdles

to get a new job with a company; this is commonly referred to as going through the employment process. Now, if a white male must jump three hurdles to get the job; a white female, four hurdles; a minority female, five hurdles, and a minority male, six hurdles, this would not be fair for those with the extra hurdles. Everyone should be subject to the same terms and rules when being considered for employment. As an interviewer, you must treat everyone the same.

Using a typical situation, let's look at what is meant by asking all applicants the same questions. Suppose you are interviewing a woman for an administrative assistant position and you have found out that she has two young children. You cannot ask her how she is going to take care of these children while she is working because you would not ask a man this question. This type of question is not related to her ability to perform her work. However, you can define the job conditions for her, explaining that she may periodically have to work overtime on short notice, or that she will be expected to work about one Saturday per month. Then, with this background, you can ask her if your job fits and meets her personal and family needs. Exactly what her child-care arrangements are is none of your concern.

Or, let's take the case of a young minority factory applicant who, as you have noticed from your office window, drives an old, dilapidated automobile. Can you ask him during the employment interview whether his car will be able to get him to and from work? Again, the answer is no, because you would not ask the same question of another applicant (who may be driving his father's new car), and the question is not related to his ability to do the job. However, you can define the hours and conditions of work, which, let's say, are 7:00 A.M. to 4:00 P.M., with overtime work as needed. You might also explain that the local bus, which goes by the plant, operates only from

6:00 A.M. to 6:00 P.M. With this background, you can then ask the young man whether he will be able to get to work on time and to get home at the end of his shift. How he will do that is his problem and not yours.

The point to keep in mind is that if you are ever called upon to defend yourself against the charge that a certain question or series of questions reduced the chances of hiring a minority or female candidate, you will have to prove that the answer given was not used as a basis for your hiring decision. You cannot create extra hurdles for some candidates, beyond those that are already laid out for other applicants. Your questions must be related only to the job, which, when you really stop to think about it, is the only fair way to treat job applicants.

INTERVIEW SMALL TALK

One of the biggest problems in the interview process is the occasional innocent question that has absolutely nothing to do with the job opening or that asks for information the employer will not use in making a hiring decision. Many times such questions are raised in the small talk at the beginning of the interview, for example: "Do you have any children?" or "What church do you attend?" Are these questions illegal? No, but if you were to use the responses to them as a reason for your employment decision, then they could be illegal.

Even if you do not use questions like these to make your decision, merely having asked them raises the possibility in the applicant's mind that the responses may have been a factor in the final decision. Litigation could well be the result of such a misconception. Again, make sure your questions are related to the applicant's ability to perform on the job.

THE INTERVIEW

We suggest that from the beginning of the interview you "set the stage" and describe the process you will follow during the interview. During the interview, ask open-ended questions that begin with *who, what, why, where,* or *how.* Open-ended questions allow you to get valuable information from the candidate and force the candidate to describe in more detail his successes and accomplishments or even his failures. This allows you the latitude to follow up with more spontaneous questions that are based upon the applicant's responses. You can do this by asking for more information, such as: "Could you tell me more?" or "Can you give me an example?" or "Could you please explain that?"

What should you do when the candidate, in an attempt to make conversation or in answering your questions, freely throws out personal information to you? Most hiring experts advise that you quickly change the subject. This is good advice; but in real life, is that the way it's always done?

This subject was discussed with a hiring manager from a company known for its high standards and low turnover. The manager said that when candidates want to "run their mouth," he lets them do so and does not try to stop or limit such talk. He explained that if you listen you may find out things about someone that will help you to make your hiring decision. He noted that what is said between two people in private is virtually impossible to challenge or verify later on. In his view, regardless of what the legal experts say, there is a reality about this process that we should not ignore or run from.

AREAS ALWAYS TO AVOID

Of course, questions should not be asked in the interview process if they elicit information about factors the employer is prohibited from considering in making an employment decision. Exhibit 7-1 specifies what you can and cannot ask in certain areas. If such information is elicited, the employer may then have a difficult task convincing a court or agency that the information was not a factor in the hiring decision. These interpretations on legal questions will apply to what you can ask when checking references, as you will see later in Chapter 15.

Although an employer cannot ask for the date of birth prior to employment, it is required on the I-9 Form after employment. However, if the position has a minimum age requirement, you can ask whether the person meets that requirement. Even though you cannot ask whether the applicant has a criminal record, you can ask whether he has ever been convicted of a crime. You should not ask about a person's health or physical condition, but you can describe the physical demands of the job. Also, the individual's fitness can be determined during the employment physical.

Exhibit 7-1. Legal inquiries before hiring.

Under federal law, there cannot be job discrimination based on sex, race, color, religion, national origin, age, or physical disability. Consequently, there are questions you should not ask a prospective employee because they may be discriminatory.

Item	You Can Ask	You Cannot Ask About
Age	Whether candidate is above minimum or below maximum age	Age, birth date, birth certificate, high school graduation date
Criminal Record	About a conviction record if it relates to ability to do the job	Arrest record
Credit Rating	Anything that directly relates to the job	Anything that does not relate to ability to do the job
Disabilities	Anything that has been proven to relate to ability to do the job	Anything that has not been proven to relate to ability to do the job
Work Schedule	About willingness to work required work schedule	Willingness to work any particular religious holiday
Marital/Family Status	Nothing	Anything
Military Record	About type of experience related to the job	Military service in any other country
National Origin	Whether candidate can legally work in the United States	Anything else
Race, Religion, Sex	Nothing	Anything

Caution: Be sure your employment policy is based on completely consistent company practices for investigating backgrounds and for making decisions not to hire. Candidates who feel they were rejected for reasons other than their qualifications may sue on grounds of discrimination. And companies that can't prove they subject every candidate to the same background investigation and the same hiring standards won't find it easy to defend themselves against such charges of discriminatory hiring practices.

Part II Summary

In Part II, you learned that:

ᛩ The choice to check the references of prospective employees is simply another business decision you must make to hire the best people for your workforce.

ᛩ The decision not to check references or not to give reference information to other employers is simply a matter of choosing not to spend the necessary time and effort to do it. This hiring activity, like all matters pertaining to employment when the law is followed as stated, presents virtually no danger to the employer.

ᛩ The law does not say that you cannot check the background of those individuals you are thinking of hiring. Many states have now passed laws that protect employers when giving out information about a past employee.

ᛩ There is a very slight danger that releasing information about a past employee could result in a lawsuit, but unless someone's basic rights have been violated, there is little chance that the suit will be successful.

⇂ The attorneys who advise employers on hiring people are somewhat isolated from the daily problems of the workplace and do not have to suffer the consequences of their advice.

Honesty—
The Best Policy

The Application
and Interview

THE EMPLOYMENT APPLICATION FORM IS the first step in establishing an honest relationship between the candidate and the employer. If a candidate attempts to deceive a prospective employer on the application itself, what will he or she lie about later? If someone will lie to get the job, he or she will probably lie to keep it.

The application serves an important purpose in the employment process. It provides the necessary data to know the candidate and what he or she brings to the table. It provides contact information and a social security number for the individual and a history of the person's life including education and work record. Prior employers should be listed, with telephone numbers for later contact as references. Of course, an application should include the applicant's signature and date signed. See Exhibit 8-1 for a sample employment application that provides all the legal and necessary information an employer needs to properly process a job applicant.

(Text continues on page 93)

Exhibit 8-1. Sample employment application.

ABC Company   EMPLOYMENT APPLICATION

In order for your application to be considered, all answers *must* be answered completely and legibly. A résumé may be attached as a supplement to the application.

ABC Company is an equal opportunity employer. All applicants will be given consideration regardless of race, color, age, religion, national origin, handicap, or veteran status.

PERSONAL DATA

PRINT NAME IN FULL				DATE
LAST	FIRST	MIDDLE	MAIDEN	

PERMANENT ADDRESS			
NUMBER & STREET	CITY	STATE	ZIP CODE

MAILING ADDRESS			
NUMBER & STREET	CITY	STATE	ZIP CODE

HOME TELEPHONE NUMBER (include area code)	WORK TELEPHONE NUMBER (include area code)	CELLULAR AND/OR PAGER NUMBER (include area code)

SOCIAL SECURITY NUMBER	ARE YOU LEGALLY ELIGIBLE TO WORK IN THE UNITED STATES? YES ☐ NO ☐	ARE YOU UNDER 18 YEARS OF AGE? YES ☐ NO ☐ IF YES GIVE DATE OF BIRTH (MM/DD/YY) / /

NAME: _____ EMPLOYMENT APPLICATION—PAGE 2

HAVE YOU EVER BEEN CONVICTED OF, OR PLED GUILTY OR NO CONTEST TO, A FELONY, MISDEMEANOR, OR ANY OFFENSE OTHER THAN A MINOR TRAFFIC VIOLATION?   YES ☐   NO ☐
(NOTE: CONVICTION OF A CRIME WILL NOT AUTOMATICALLY DISQUALIFY YOU FROM FURTHER CONSIDERATION FOR EMPLOYMENT.)
IF YES
IN WHAT COUNTY AND STATE DID IT OCCUR?: _____   YEAR _____

PARTICULARS REGARDING THE CONVICTION: _____

POSITION OR TYPE OF WORK DESIRED:	SALARY EXPECTED PER MONTH:	DATE OF AVAILABILITY:

HOW WERE YOU REFERRED TO ABC COMPANY?	HAVE YOU EVER APPLIED PREVIOUSLY TO ABC COMPANY?	HAVE YOU EVER BEEN EMPLOYED WITH ABC COMPANY?
	WHERE? WHEN?	WHERE? WHEN?

RELATIVES OR ACQUAINTANCES EMPLOYED BY ABC COMPANY

NAME: _____   RELATIONSHIP: _____

NAME: _____   RELATIONSHIP: _____

NAME: _____   RELATIONSHIP: _____

UNITED STATES MILITARY SERVICE	BRANCH	RANK	TYPE OF DISCHARGE
FROM ___ TO ___			

PREVIOUS RESIDENCES IN THE LAST 10 YEARS	FROM (month/year)	TO (month/year)
STREET _____		
CITY _____ STATE __ ZIP ___		

(continues)

Exhibit 8-1. (*continued*)

NAME: _____   EMPLOYMENT APPLICATION—PAGE 3

STREET _____		
CITY _____ STATE __ ZIP _____		
STREET _____		
CITY _____ STATE __ ZIP _____		

EDUCATION

SCHOOL	NAME AND ADDRESS	COURSE OR MAJOR AREA OF STUDY	YEARS COMPLETED DEGREE(S)
HIGH SCHOOL			
COLLEGE			
GRADUATE			
BUSINESS			
TRADE			
OTHER			

UNDER WHAT NAME DID YOU GRADUATE FROM HIGH SCHOOL? _____

UNDER WHAT NAME DID YOU GRADUATE FROM COLLEGE: _____

IF YOU RECEIVED A G.E.D., PLEASE ANSWER THE FOLLOWING:

TESTING SITE: _____   APPROXIMATE YEAR: _____

CITY/STATE: _____

NAME: _____ EMPLOYMENT APPLICATION—PAGE 4

SPECIAL QUALIFICATIONS

NAME ANY PROFESSIONAL ORGANIZATIONS TO WHICH YOU BELONG:

_____

HAVE YOU EVER HAD ANY PROFESSIONAL REGISTRATION, LICENSE, OR
CERTIFICATION SUSPENDED OR REVOKED?
YES ☐   NO ☐

IF YES PLEASE STATE PARTICULARS SURROUNDING THE SUSPENSION OR
REVOCATION:

_____

_____

_____

LIST TYPE OF SKILL, MACHINES, AND PROFICIENCY (WHERE APPLICABLE):

_____

CLERICAL (TYPING, WORD PROCESSING, STENOGRAPHY, SOFTWARE, ETC.)

_____

ELECTRONIC DATA-PROCESSING EQUIPMENT (COMPUTERS, TERMINALS, CRTs,
ETC.)

_____

LANGUAGES (INDICATE ABILITY TO READ, WRITE, OR SPEAK)

_____

OTHER

ARE THERE ANY REASONS WHY YOU MAY NOT BE ABLE TO PERFORM THE
ESSENTIAL ELEMENTS OF THE JOB FOR WHICH YOU ARE APPLYING?
YES ☐   NO ☐

IF YES, PLEASE DESCRIBE: _____

_____

(continues)

Exhibit 8-1. (*continued*)

NAME: _____   EMPLOYMENT APPLICATION—PAGE 5

ARE YOU CURRENTLY EMPLOYED?   YES ☐   NO ☐
(IF YES, ANSWER A, B, C, & D)

A. WOULD CONTACTING YOUR PRESENT SUPERVISOR/EMPLOYER JEOPARDIZE
   YOUR CURRENT POSITION?   YES ☐   NO ☐

B. IS YOUR IMMEDIATE SUPERVISOR/EMPLOYER AWARE THAT YOU ARE SEEKING
   OTHER EMPLOYMENT?   YES ☐   NO ☐

C. HAVE YOU ALREADY GIVEN NOTICE TO YOUR PRESENT EMPLOYER?
                                                   YES ☐   NO ☐

D. MAY WE CONTACT YOUR IMMEDIATE SUPERVISOR/EMPLOYER?
                                                   YES ☐   NO ☐

EMPLOYMENT HISTORY

INSTRUCTIONS:

1. BEGIN WITH YOUR PRESENT OR MOST RECENT EMPLOYER AND WORK
   BACKWARD CHRONOLOGICALLY.

2. INCLUDE ALL PRIOR POSITIONS HELD DURING THE LAST 10 YEARS, FOR
   WHOM YOU HAVE WORKED EITHER FULL-TIME OR PART-TIME.

3. FOR ANY PERIOD OF UNEMPLOYMENT, ON A SEPARATE SHEET, DESCRIBE,
   GIVE DATES AND REASONS, AND ATTACH TO THIS APPLICATION.

4. DO NOT STATE "REFER TO RÉSUMÉ."

5. USE ADDITIONAL SHEETS IF NECESSARY.

NAME: _____ EMPLOYMENT APPLICATION—PAGE 6

	DATES EMPLOYED (MM/YY)
NAME OF EMPLOYER	FROM: _____
ADDRESS OF EMPLOYER	TO: _____
NUMBER AND STREET	BASE SALARY OR HOURLY RATE START: END:
CITY STATE ZIP ( ) _____ PHONE NUMBER (including area code)	OTHER COMPENSATION (bonus, overtime, etc.)
NATURE OF BUSINESS	

EXACT TITLE OF YOUR POSITION: _____

DESCRIBE YOUR DUTIES AND ACCOMPLISHMENTS: _____

_____

NAME AND TITLE OF IMMEDIATE SUPERVISOR: _____

PHONE NUMBER THIS PERSON CAN BE REACHED AT: (   ) _____
(including area code)

MAY WE CONTACT?   YES ☐   NO ☐

REASON FOR LEAVING: _____

_____

(continues)

Exhibit 8-1. (*continued*)

NAME: _____   EMPLOYMENT APPLICATION—PAGE 7

_____ NAME OF EMPLOYER	DATES EMPLOYED (MM/YY) FROM: _____
_____ ADDRESS OF EMPLOYER	TO: _____
_____ NUMBER AND STREET	BASE SALARY OR HOURLY RATE
_____ CITY STATE ZIP	START: END:
( ) _____ PHONE NUMBER (including area code)	OTHER COMPENSATION (bonus, overtime, etc.)
_____ NATURE OF BUSINESS	

EXACT TITLE OF YOUR POSITION: _____

DESCRIBE YOUR DUTIES AND ACCOMPLISHMENTS: _____

_____

NAME AND TITLE OF IMMEDIATE SUPERVISOR: _____

PHONE NUMBER THIS PERSON CAN BE REACHED AT: ( ) _____
                                             (including area code)

MAY WE CONTACT?   YES ☐   NO ☐

REASON FOR LEAVING: _____

_____

NAME: _____   EMPLOYMENT APPLICATION—PAGE 8

	DATES EMPLOYED (MM/YY)
NAME OF EMPLOYER	FROM: _____
ADDRESS OF EMPLOYER	TO: _____
NUMBER AND STREET	BASE SALARY OR HOURLY RATE
CITY **STATE** **ZIP**	START: END:
( ) _____ **PHONE NUMBER (including area code)**	OTHER COMPENSATION (bonus, overtime, etc.)
NATURE OF BUSINESS	

EXACT TITLE OF YOUR POSITION: _____

DESCRIBE YOUR DUTIES AND ACCOMPLISHMENTS: _____

_____

NAME AND TITLE OF IMMEDIATE SUPERVISOR: _____

PHONE NUMBER THIS PERSON CAN BE REACHED AT: ( ) _____
(including area code)

MAY WE CONTACT?   YES ☐   NO ☐

REASON FOR LEAVING: _____

_____

(continues)

Exhibit 8-1. (*continued*)

NAME: _____   EMPLOYMENT APPLICATION—PAGE 9

REFERENCES

LIST 3 PREVIOUS SUPERVISORS WHO CAN OBJECTIVELY ASSESS YOUR PROFESSIONAL PERFORMANCE (do not include current supervisor)				
NAME	COMPANY	TITLE/ RELATIONSHIP YEARS KNOWN	BUSINESS TELEPHONE (including area code)	HOME TELEPHONE (including area code)

LIST 3 PREVIOUS COWORKERS WHO CAN OBJECTIVELY ASSESS YOUR PROFESSIONAL PERFORMANCE (include 1 current coworker)				
NAME	COMPANY	TITLE/ RELATIONSHIP YEARS KNOWN	BUSINESS TELEPHONE (including area code)	HOME TELEPHONE (including area code)

LIST 3 PEOPLE WHO REPORTED TO YOU WHO CAN OBJECTIVELY ASSESS YOUR PROFESSIONAL PERFORMANCE (may include current employees)				
NAME	COMPANY	TITLE/ RELATIONSHIP YEARS KNOWN	BUSINESS TELEPHONE (including area code)	HOME TELEPHONE (including area code)

NAME: _____ EMPLOYMENT APPLICATION—PAGE 10

LIST 2 PERSONAL REFERENCES (close friends or acquaintances)				
NAME	COMPANY	TITLE/ RELATIONSHIP YEARS KNOWN	BUSINESS TELEPHONE (including area code)	HOME TELEPHONE (including area code)

IMPORTANT: READ CAREFULLY BEFORE SIGNING.

AS AN APPLICANT, YOUR SIGNATURE INDICATES THAT YOU AGREE TO AND UNDERSTAND THE FOLLOWING:

- I certify that the information that I have provided on this application is true, correct, and complete. I understand that any misleading information, omission, or falsification is grounds for rejection or my dismissal from the company.
- I authorize all schools, companies, corporations, credit bureaus, law enforcement agencies, and my present and/ or prior employer to furnish ABC Company with their record of my services, employment background, character, qualifications, reason for leaving, and any other information they may have concerning me. I release all parties from all liability for any damages in furnishing this information.
- I understand that if employed, my employment is for no definite period and that I may terminate my employment relationship at any time, for any reason, and that ABC Company has the same right, applicable to all federal and state laws.
- I further understand that all applicants are subject to a medical examination, including an alcohol, drug, and substance screening and that any offer of employment will be

(continues)

Exhibit 8-1. *(continued)*

NAME: _____   EMPLOYMENT APPLICATION—PAGE 11

contingent upon satisfactory results of such examinations' inquiries and screening. Examinations are to be made by a physician designated by the company.

■ If employed, I promise, as a condition of employment, that I will within three (3) days of starting work submit verification of my U.S. employment eligibility as required by law on INS Form I-9 or its successor form.

■ I agree that if I am employed by ABC Company, a full transcript of my records as an employee, including reason for separation or termination, may be given to a prospective future employer on request and do hereby release ABC Company from any and all liability or damages resulting in furnishing this information.

■ I understand that the completion of this application form does not guarantee my employment with ABC Company, does not indicate that there is a position available, and in no way obligates the company.

The below signed applicant hereby acknowledges that he or she has carefully read and understands and agrees to the above.

Applicant Signature: _____   Date: _____

Applicant Printed Signature: _____

THE INTERVIEW ITSELF

When we teach interviewing, we recommend the behavioral-based method of gathering information from the candidate. In this technique, the candidate is asked to talk about specific achievements or situations in his or her work career. Sometimes this is also called behavioral-event or behavioral-incident questioning.

This technique involves asking simple, probing questions until you can clearly see the situation or incident in your own mind. Make the applicant relate in vivid detail his or her specific achievements. In other words, get sound evidence through examples, facts, statistics, and cases where and when such behavior occurred. For example, when discussing attendance, you want the applicant to cite figures, as in the statement "I only missed two days and I was late three times last year." Demand evidence for anything that is said. It is all based on the simple premise that actions speak louder than words.

"Please give me an example." These are the five most important words in the interviewer's arsenal, and they cannot be used too often. The main purpose of an interview is to gather stories—that is, practical illustrations of how things worked out (or didn't). You can almost measure your effectiveness by the number of "sagas" an interview produces.

Instead of asking questions such as: "Are you a good leader?" or "Tell me about yourself," ask for specific achievements and accomplishments. For example, say to the applicant, "Describe to me an actual situation in which you were a strong leader," or "Tell me with specific examples why you think you are better than the other candidates we are talking to." The key is to listen actively so that you understand what action was taken and then learn what the end result was.

Employers are increasingly using behavioral interviewing. It emphasizes behavior, not general statements. By having the candidate cite specific examples of past performance, interviewers can anticipate the candidate's future behavior on the job. You will then be able to confirm the validity of this information when references are contacted.

It is amazing how some interviewers, including hiring specialists, think that they can tell whether or not someone is a good candidate merely by looking at the person. There is still a lot of prejudice, ignorance, and misunderstanding by those hiring authorities who think they can judge a person's competency by his or her appearance or mannerisms.

We are reminded of an employment interviewer we worked with who noted that the candidate for an accounting position had terrible presentation skills and recommended that the individual be dropped from consideration. This observation and conclusion were based on the male candidate's lack of good eye contact and stumbling speech pattern. However, the hiring manager ignored these characteristics and focused primarily on the person's technical qualifications, past experience, and performance record and hired the person anyway. Within a year, he was a top performer and was promoted.

The hiring manager had carefully assessed the skills that were needed, noting that she was not looking for a smooth interview but whether the candidate had the necessary qualifications for the job. The lesson here is that a candidate should be judged on proven and past performance not only on his or her interviewing skills.

IDENTIFYING REFERENCES

The most feared words a candidate can hear are, "We are going to check your references." This means quite simply,

"Be totally honest with us. Distorting your background won't fly here, and only the truth will work in getting the job." Many employers are now having applicants sign an employment release (meeting the requirements of the Fair Credit Reporting Act—see Chapter 11) before being considered for employment (see Exhibit 8-2). This form not only states that references will be checked, but the applicant, by signing the form, gives full permission to check his or her background. Most attorneys advise that employers have the best protection from lawsuits if the applicant signs a clear release that allows the company to check his or her background and to contact references. If this is set forth in a separate document, rather than by the usual sign-off at the bottom of the employment application, it constitutes a much stronger legal document.

The interview is the most appropriate place in which to identify references. We cannot tell you how many times we have received reference-checking assignments in our private practice in which the client company did not provide the names of the people it would like us to contact. The hiring managers have spent hours or even days interviewing and getting to know a prospective employee; yet they are unable to identify one significant person in the candidate's work life that we should talk to about the candidate. They have completely missed the opportunity to identify knowledgeable people who can either verify or refute the information furnished by the applicant.

Two Principles to Ponder

As already explained, job seekers are well aware that what they say will probably never be checked out. Most employers leave it up to the candidate to list the people he or she would like contacted as references. The process is slanted toward the applicant, and this needs to be

Exhibit 8-2. Authorization to release information.

AUTHORIZATION FOR RELEASE OF INFORMATION FOR EMPLOYMENT PURPOSES

I hereby authorize [*insert company name*], and its designated agents and representatives, to conduct a comprehensive review of my background, causing a consumer report and/or an investigative report to be generated for employment purposes.

I understand that the scope of the consumer report/investigative report may include, but is not limited to, the following areas:

> Verification of social security number; current and previous residences; employment history, including all personnel files, education, character references, credit history and reports; criminal history records from any criminal justice agency in any or all federal, state, and county jurisdictions; birth records; motor vehicle records to include traffic citations and registration; and any other public records.

I authorize the complete release of these records or data pertaining to me that an individual, company, firm, corporation, or public agency may have. I understand that I must provide my date of birth to adequately complete said screening, and acknowledge that my date of birth will not affect any hiring decisions.

I hereby release [*insert company name*], and its agents, officials, representatives, or assigned agencies, including officers, employees, or related personnel both individually and collectively, from any and all liability for damages of whatever kind, which may at any time result to me, my heirs, family or associates because of compliance with this authorization and re-lease. You may contact me as indicated below.

I understand this authorization will not expire if I am hired, but also understand I have the right to revoke the authorization at any time, provided I do so in writing.

Print Name: _____
       (First)   (Middle)   (Last)   (Maiden)

Date of Birth	Social Security Number
Street Address	City and State
Driver's License Number	State of Issue
Signature	Date

changed. Let's analyze the interview in its entirety, starting with two points that should be kept in mind if the interview is to be made a more meaningful exercise for the employer.

First Principle

Let the applicant know up front that references will be checked. This statement will go a long way toward making the individual see the need to be honest during the interview. Then, during the interview itself, insist on honest answers from the job applicant by making statements such as the following:

1. Answer the question the way you think your references will.

2. When we call your references, what do you think
   they will say?
3. With whom should I talk to verify this point?

Our conscience works best when we know that we
are being watched. What happens when we are driving
down the highway and we see a police officer up ahead?
Almost by instinct, we lift our foot from the gas pedal,
immediately glance at the speedometer, and probably put
our foot on the brake. Or, what happens in a classroom
when the teacher leaves the room? Usually, the students
start misbehaving.

By giving a warning at the beginning, and during the
interview, you have a tremendous influence on keeping
the applicant honest. You remain in control during the
interview and are able to gain information necessary to
validate what the candidate has told you.

Second Principle

Identify and gather the names of meaningful references during the interview. How do you do this? Again, it
is very simple: During the interview, you identify the key
players in the applicant's work life and write down their
names. When you have identified a previous supervisor,
ask the candidate whether this person is still employed by
the company and the telephone number he can be
reached at. In other words, choose the references you
want to speak with and not the references the applicant
would prefer that you contact.

This is the only realistic way to identify references
that will provide you with the information necessary for
your hiring decision. If you allow the candidate to choose
his references, you may end up with his best friend, his
in-laws, or his minister. This is not to imply that these
individuals will not be honest and reliable, but they prob-

ably have not worked directly with the candidate and do not have knowledge of his work ethic or skills and abilities on the job.

We can usually tell whether the candidate whose references we are going to check has a strong work record just by looking at the references given. If the references are previous managers, company officials, or other important people in her work life, then this person is proud of her work history and is not afraid of what these people will say when contacted. If the names given are those of close friends, relatives, or others who have never really worked with the candidate, we often find that she has something to hide.

What do you do in the case of a person who has been out of the job force for a while or may just be entering the job market? Chances are this person has been affiliated with a group or organization or may have worked as a volunteer. Find out the names of people the person worked with in the organization and contact these people. These references have had direct contact with the candidate and will be able to provide you with information about how the candidate performed his or her duties and responsibilities.

There is no reason not to identify at least six references during the interview. Get the names of the applicant's boss and the boss's boss, the names of two peers, and the names of two subordinates or other persons below the level of the candidate at every place the candidate has worked. We call it the $2 + 2 + 2 = 6$. Obviously, you can do the same thing by adding $1 + 1 + 1 = 3$ or $3 + 3 + 3 = 9$. The point is that it is not difficult to develop key references during the interview for each one of the applicant's past employers (see Exhibit 8-3).

THE INTERVIEW IN PERSPECTIVE

As previously discussed, a common mistake interviewers make is talking too much. As an interviewer, you must

Exhibit 8-3. Hot tips.

It is important that the applicant's last direct supervisor (from each employer) be pursued for a reference. The last supervisor is the most qualified person to provide details surrounding the candidate's job responsibilities, level of performance, as well as the circumstances surrounding his or her separation. It is the applicant's obligation to provide you with the names of these individuals. If he or she does not volunteer this information, ask for it.

learn the art of engaging another person silently. Remaining silent is difficult for most interviewers, but the general rule is that the person being interviewed should do about 80 percent of the talking.

A related mistake is that of adopting a free-floating conversational interview style. This allows the candidate to discuss her experience largely on her own terms and makes it difficult to compare candidates. For the purpose of comparing responses across individuals, it is best to use a semistructured approach in which provisions are made for follow-up questions as needed. A detailed inquiry or a persistent follow-up on an initially general question can bring out critical information about the candidate.

Do not stop digging until you fully understand the information you are being told. Do not be afraid to ask what might seem like a dumb question to get the answers you need. Watch the candidate's body language and any signs of hesitancy in answering a question. If you feel someone may not have been truthful with you, reword the question and ask him to go over the details again. Remember that your job is to ask questions, which means any kind of question that is necessary to know the real job candidate. Think small. You are after the details of someone's work life.

A detailed, semistructured interview should not be a

stress-inducing exercise. Some managers conduct stress interviews, believing that this will allow them to observe how the candidate copes with stress. The problem is that in most cases, the stress produced by this approach is quite different from the stress produced by the job. A little anxiety in the candidate is fine, but deliberately setting up the applicant to feel unusual stress serves no good purpose.

As with a good detective, your purpose during the interview is not to make a friend but to get the facts. Keep asking the applicant to talk about what she actually did— her day-to-day activities, short-term or long-term projects, and ultimate achievements. Notice what she is wearing, her tone of voice, even when she smiles. When you finally go over the questions, you may be surprised at the patterns and clues that emerge.

Identifying and gathering references during the interview may be stressful for a candidate who has something to hide. Good candidates will have no problem with this. In fact, they will see you as an interviewer who is in control and knows what you are doing. They will view the company as one that wants to ensure that the people it hires are qualified for their positions. They will welcome the opportunity for you to speak with the many fine people they have helped and worked with. A poor applicant would rather keep control and steer you to the references of his choosing.

Squeezing every ounce of usable information you can out of the interview is just good business. It not only provides you with the information you need to make an informed hiring decision but also prevents problems in the future. Hiring someone without asking difficult questions and not performing a reference check is asking for trouble. If this person is let go after a few months on the job, an enormous amount of time will have been wasted training the individual, not to mention the money wasted in wages. Any interviewing method that does not include identifying and checking references is not in tune with what is needed in today's business environment.

Finally, a word about interview impressions: Try as you may to conduct an objective evaluation, an interview is essentially an emotional event. Subjective reactions, whether conscious or unconscious, are inevitable. To clear up any doubts you may have, call those persons (references) who have been closely involved on the job with the applicant and who can provide further insight into the person. With this information, the odds are that you will make the correct hiring decision.

Some companies are now using a separate background questionnaire that is completed by the applicant prior to the interview (see Exhibit 8-4). The purpose of this questionnaire is to get basic behavioral information from the candidate before the interview itself and thus save precious interviewing time. In addition, it tends to keep the candidate honest. If a separate form is not used, you may want to ask some of these questions during the interview itself.

INTERVIEWING QUESTIONS

The short interviewing format (see Exhibit 8-5) can be used to interview hourly or entry-level applicants. It has corresponding reference-checking questions (short version), shown in Exhibit 15-5, that match the interviewing questions. Many employers have used these two forms with great effectiveness.

The long interviewing format (see Exhibit 8-6) is appropriate for higher-level openings. Review these twenty questions and decide on those you want to use for the opening you have. You may decide to use some of the questions for a lower-level opening and all of them for a key position. Feel free to substitute or to add questions of

Exhibit 8-4. Sample background questionnaire.

LMN CORPORATION
109 Aurora Way
Denver, Colorado

Your background and work history will be discussed with you during your interview. Please answer all questions with a yes or no prior to the interview.

	Yes	No
1. Have you ever been placed on probation or terminated for poor job performance?	___	___
2. Have you ever been disciplined or fired for insubordination?	___	___
3. Have you ever been disciplined or discharged for violating a safety rule(s)?	___	___
4. Have you ever been disciplined or terminated for absenteeism, tardiness, failure to notify your company when absent, or any other attendance-related reason?	___	___
5. Have you ever been disciplined or discharged for theft, unauthorized removal of company property, or related offenses?	___	___
6. Have you ever been disciplined or fired for fighting, assault, or similar offenses?	___	___
7. Have you ever been disciplined or discharged for being under the influence of alcohol or drugs, or for the possession, use, or abuse of alcohol or drugs?	___	___
8. Have you ever been convicted of a crime?	___	___

I certify that the above answers are true to the best of my knowledge. I understand that any falsification discovered before or after I am employed may be cause for my being disqualified or removed from employment with the company.

_____   _____
(Candidate's Signature)   (Date)

_____
(Social Security Number)

Exhibit 8-5. Interview questions (short form).

Look for someone you can be enthusiastic about. Beyond your gut feeling, make sure the applicant is qualified for your opening. Use these key questions for all the candidates you interview for the position:

- ৭ How long did you work for your last employer? Why did you leave? How about the employer before that? [*Go back at least five to ten years.*]
- ৭ Specifically, what did you do for your last employer(s)?
- ৭ What were your accomplishments? What changed as a result of your being employed there?
- ৭ What are your strengths as you see them? Would your friends agree?
- ৭ What former bosses, coworkers, or subordinates can I call for references? [*Get at least five names.*]
- ৭ What do you feel separates you from other applicants for our opening?
- ৭ What can we expect from you if you come to work for us?

A final word of advice: Use common sense, as you would for any kind of decision. Look for solid evidence that the person you choose can increase your unit's performance and really help your operation.

your own. This form and the longer reference checklists in Chapter 15 provide the basis for a power interview and thorough reference checking.

Good questions are the foundation of a good interview. The right questions, when properly used and followed up on, will uncover the information you seek from a job candidate.

Exhibit 8-6. Interview questions (long form).

Explain to your candidate:

"I will ask you general questions that provide an opportunity for you to tell me your specific career achievements to date, as well as your future expectations. I am going to be concentrating on your relevant work experience, knowledge, and competence.

"I will also ask you to provide the names of references you feel will share with me their views regarding your career progress. This is important because I may want to contact specific individuals who can verify what we have spoken about during the interview."

Ask your candidate:

1. Why are you interested in this position?
   Subquestions (if necessary):
   ৭ How did you get into this type of work?
   ৭ Why are you interested in making a career move now?

2. What specific attributes do you possess that will make you effective in this position?
   Subquestions (if necessary):
   ৭ What unique talents will you bring to us?
   ৭ How much do you know about our position opening?

3. What is your definition of career success?
   Subquestions (if necessary):
   ৭ How will you know when you have become successful?
   ৭ What would you like to be earning in the years ahead?

(continues)

Exhibit 8-6. (*continued*)

4. How has your previous job performance been appraised in terms of specific pluses and minuses?
   Subquestions (if necessary):
   ? What three areas of your job do you like the most? Least?
   ? What recent accomplishments are you most proud of?
   ? Whom can I contact to discuss this with (if needed)?
   Name _____ Phone _____ Company _____

5. Describe a situation in which you felt particularly effective.
   Subquestions (if necessary):
   ? What is the most important idea you implemented in your present/last job?
   ? What was your single most important contribution to your present/last employer?
   ? Who would have knowledge of this action (if needed)?
   Name _____ Phone _____ Company _____

6. Describe a time when you felt ineffective and explain exactly what you did about it.
   Subquestions (if necessary):
   ? What did you learn from this experience?
   ? What was the biggest mistake you ever made in your working career?
   ? Who would have knowledge of this occurrence (if needed)?
   Name _____ Phone _____ Company _____

7. What qualities have you liked or disliked in your previous bosses?
   Subquestions (if necessary):
   ? Who was the strongest boss you ever had? The weakest?

৭ Do you prefer to work for a delegator or for one who gives you close supervision?
৭ Who was your last boss? Can we contact him/her (if needed)?
Name _____ Phone _____ Company _____

8. How many employees have you supervised in your past assignment(s)?
What has been the group's overall level of performance?
Subquestions (if necessary):
৭ Describe how you influence or motivate others.
৭ Do you like being in charge of people?
৭ Whom should I speak with to review this information (if needed)?
Name _____ Phone _____ Company _____

9. Have you had direct hiring authority? Have those you hired worked out?
Subquestions (if necessary):
৭ What do you look for in a job applicant?
৭ What do other people think about the people you hire?
৭ Who would have knowledge of this area (if needed)?
Name _____ Phone _____ Company _____

10. Give me an example of your having cut the costs, improved the efficiency, or eliminated unnecessary work in your daily activities.
Subquestions (if necessary):
৭ What was the most satisfying thing you ever did?
৭ Have you ever received an award or a citation?
৭ Whom can I discuss this with (if needed)?
Name _____ Phone _____ Company _____

(continues)

Exhibit 8-6. (*continued*)

11. Have you been a reliable employee? Can you give
    specific examples to illustrate this?
    Subquestions (if necessary):
    ٩ How many times were you absent in the past
    year? Year before?
    ٩ How often have you changed jobs? Moved or re-
    located?
    ٩ Whom can I discuss this with (if needed)?
    Name _____ Phone _____ Company _____

12. How well do you interact with supervisors, peers,
    and subordinates?
    Subquestions (if necessary):
    ٩ In what manner do you communicate with your
    subordinates? With superiors?
    ٩ Describe a time in which you worked on a team
    or in a group and tell me what role you played in
    that group.
    ٩ Whom can I talk with about this (if needed)?
    Name _____ Phone _____ Company _____

13. What would be the advantage of a new company
    hiring you?
    Subquestions (if necessary):
    ٩ Describe the best company you ever worked for.
    ٩ What is the biggest single problem your current/
    past company had?
    ٩ Who would be able to discuss this with me (if
    needed)?
    Name _____ Phone _____ Company _____

14. What, in your opinion, is your future growth poten-
    tial? How far can you go?
    Subquestions (if necessary):
    ٩ How have you changed over the past five years?

ᠻ What would other people say about your potential?

ᠻ Who would be the best person to talk with about this (if needed)?
Name _____ Phone _____ Company _____

15. How are you best managed?
Subquestions (if necessary):
ᠻ What do you expect from a manager?
ᠻ What was your favorite manager like?
ᠻ Is there someone who would be helpful to us in this regard (if needed)?
Name _____ Phone _____ Company _____

16. What is your single strongest characteristic and your greatest weakness? What are you doing to build on that strength? And what are you doing to reduce the weakness?
Subquestions (if necessary):
ᠻ In what areas of your present job are you strongest? Weakest?
ᠻ In the past year, what classes, seminars, or conferences have you attended? How many were at your own expense?
ᠻ Whom may we talk with to better understand this (if needed)?
Name _____ Phone _____ Company _____

17. What mistakes have you made in your career?
Subquestions (if necessary):
ᠻ Have you ever been reprimanded?
ᠻ Have you ever been fired?
ᠻ Who would have knowledge of this area (if needed)?
Name _____ Phone _____ Company _____

18. What was the most difficult ethical decision you ever had to make?
Subquestions (if necessary):
ᠻ How do you define ethics?
ᠻ What is unethical behavior?

(continues)

Exhibit 8-6. (*continued*)

19. Is there anything in your background that you are not particularly proud of, that you'd rather talk about now than have discovered during our reference checking?
    Subquestions (if necessary):
    ৎ What will your current/previous employer say about you?
    ৎ Have any of your employers ever refused to provide a reference for you?

20. Is there anything more you would like to contribute to the interview?

Advise the candidate:

"At times I may find it valuable to speak with other persons your references may refer me to. Are there any restrictions as to whom I may contact? If so, please explain why and give me their names and the companies where they work."

Name _____ Company _____

Name _____ Company _____

Spotting Liars

LYING IS NOTHING MORE THAN someone trying to make things the way he or she wants them to be rather than the way things actually are. When people lie, their actions will often give them away.

There are two types of lies:

1. *Prepared lies or false statements planned ahead of time.* People who tell prepared lies tend to give brief answers, have tremors in their voices, or sound rehearsed.
2. *Spontaneous lies, or false responses to an unexpected question.* People who tell spontaneous lies tend to give brief answers (most liars can't think of what to say quickly enough), make speaking errors such as "we was," or resort to meaningless phrases such as "you know what I mean."

There are two primary ways to lie:

1. *To conceal.* In concealing, the liar withholds information without actually saying anything untrue.

2. *To falsify.* In falsifying, the liar presents false information as if it were true.

The best way to determine whether someone is lying is to ask him or her to elaborate on the statement. Most liars do not want to go into detail and they hate to keep adding to their lies. When asked to provide more details, most people will stumble around or completely freeze up. Not every little miscue means that someone is lying (people are nervous in interview situations, after all), but if you suspect someone is not being truthful, press harder to see whether that is the case. If he or she is not lying, no one will be the worse off and both of you will probably have gained more faith in each other as the result of the probing.

Of course, the best way to determine whether someone is not being completely honest with you during the interview process is through reference checking. These checks, if done properly, will validate that what you have been told and led to believe by the applicant is, in fact, true and accurate. It makes sense in today's world, where lying can be commonplace, to check out what people tell you.

AGGRESSIVE LISTENING

If you listen to and observe people carefully, they will tell you almost everything you want or need to know to make enlightened decisions. Even though people are often inconsistent, they will reveal themselves in time if they are given the opportunity to speak. However, you must first know how to be a good listener. Remember the 80/20 rule—the applicant should do 80 percent of the talking during the interview and the person conducting the interview should talk only 20 percent of the time.

When interviewing someone or checking references, it is critical that you hear what is actually being said. Most interviewers will miss the information being supplied because they are thinking about what question they are going to ask next rather than listening to what the person being interviewed is saying. Instead of mentally rehearsing the next point on your agenda or the next question you wish to ask, listen and respond spontaneously. Probe, question, and follow up until you are fully satisfied with the answers you have been given and feel reasonably confident that what you have heard is true. In other words, never stop questioning until you have all the information you seek.

You must pay attention not only to what is being said but also to how it is said. By this, we mean voice expression, underlying intent, or any hidden clues. Stop for a moment and think of an important conversation you have had recently in which there were some underlying or special cues from the speaker that were critical to understanding the message being given. Examples of such cues may include a clearing of the throat, a nervous laugh, or a long pause. You probably noticed these cues because they were so open and apparent. The secret to successful interviewing is to be able to pick up on clues that may not be so obvious—which are there if you are alert enough to catch them.

Show the candidate you are listening. Look at his or her face. Lean a little toward the person. These seemingly small body language signals tell someone you are interested in what he or she has to say. Concentrate on the person's voice. As the person speaks, think about what is being said. Above all, do not think about what you are going to say in response to the applicant's comments before he or she finishes speaking. If you are thinking about your next question, you cannot listen to what that person is saying at the moment. You can easily miss an important point, or even worse, you may miss a crucial clue about the candidate's honesty.

We have found that one of the most potent ways to draw someone out in an interview is to pause or use silence. This technique usually makes the candidate uncomfortable, and he or she may then try to fill the void by providing more information. Anxiety makes people uncomfortable and most people will try to put someone at ease if they sense that another person is nervous or apprehensive. However, if you can learn to allow the other person to be anxious, you may discover some important information that you would otherwise have missed. Television interviewers and police officers use this technique with great effectiveness. Watch one of the well-known and highly competent network TV hosts ask a guest a thoughtful question—and then be completely quiet until it is answered. Try it during your next interview or simply in a conversation with someone. You'll be surprised at how most people simply cannot stand the sudden quiet and will rush to give you more details.

Finally, ask the applicant to name other people who can verify the information he or she has given you. This is absolutely critical for two reasons:

1. It tends to keep the respondent honest.
2. It provides sources to contact who will validate what you have been told by the candidate and other references.

Most training for interviewers emphasizes strong questioning techniques. Although the proper questions are vital to a good interview, too few interviewers know how to listen effectively, and therefore, most never actually hear what candidates are telling them.

Speak less, listen more. If you'll allow them to, people will go to great lengths to explain why they think, feel, and act the way they do. And that information will help you to make a better hiring decision.

KEEPING THE APPLICANT HONEST

We have always heard that honesty is the best policy. But how do you convince job applicants of this? In the United States, a new trend has developed toward being a "nice interviewer." Many hiring managers, who either do not want to offend a candidate or are not properly trained, ask easy and sometimes pointless questions rather than the difficult or meaningful ones that would elicit the applicant's deepest thoughts, feelings, and abilities.

The trouble with this type of interviewing is that these nice people become sitting ducks for all the dishonest applicants crowding the job market today. We all know there are individuals who will say anything as long as it helps them to get the job. When you are evaluating someone for employment, your role is not to make a new friend but to ensure that your company is hiring the right person. You don't have to be rough and tough to do this; in fact, being tough does not guarantee that you won't get fooled. What best protects you from being taken advantage of is being in complete control during the entire hiring process.

What we advocate in handling and screening employees is a style midway between being nice and tough. That is, always treat candidates fairly and firmly—right down to the words, phrases, and mannerisms you use. You need to take control from the start and stay in control. For some of you this will require that you become more tough minded than you have been. But if you do what we recommend, it will become quite easy to stay in charge all the way through the hiring process. Success comes from being in complete control of any situation.

How Honest Are You?

We have discussed how important it is to insist on and get honest answers from job applicants. But honesty is a two-way street. Are you being honest with your prospective employees? Whether it is unintentional or deliberate, misinforming candidates is a mistake recruiters should not make. You need to be completely honest with the candidates so that they can make an informed, conscious decision about whether the position is right for them. Do not tell them what you think they want to hear.

Have an up-to-date and accurate job description for the candidate to review. Often, an applicant may decline to interview for a position after seeing the job requirements. Once hired, this employee should be given a copy of the job description so that he or she has a clear understanding of the organization's work expectations.

The job description should state in detail the essential functions the person in the position will be required to perform, as well as any duties that are performed occasionally. You also want to define the personal characteristics that the job requires. This would include knowledge and experience factors, as well as educational, motivational, and personality factors. Avoid stereotyping that would eliminate qualified people for consideration.

You can refer to the job description when speaking with references to ensure that the candidate can perform the functions of the job. A well-written job description will also help you to defeat discrimination claims against your company (see Exhibit 9-1).

Candidates know—sometimes sooner, sometimes later—when a company has not been on the up-and-up with them. They will catch on, and when they do, the result may be as simple as a job offer rejection or as complex as a lawsuit. Misrepresentation claims are brought

---

Exhibit 9-1. Job description.

What information should be included in a job description?

General Position Information:

1. Date description was written
2. Job title, department, and location
3. Reporting relationship
4. Job classification (i.e., exempt versus nonexempt)
5. Approved by and date

Job Duties and Responsibilities:

1. Summary of job
2. Essential duties and responsibilities
3. Additional duties and responsibilities
4. Supervisor responsibilities (if applicable)

Special Requirements:

1. Education and/or experience
2. Language skills
3. Mathematical skills
4. Reasoning ability
   Tools or equipment to be used
   Skills required
   Certificates, licenses, registrations
   Physical demands and work environment
   Behavior/personality traits

---

against former employers often enough to be a potentially costly problem.

For example, say you ask an applicant why she left her last job, and she says, "I couldn't stand my boss. He was dictatorial, never had a good word for anyone, and cursed at people." Now if this describes almost exactly what her new boss in your company will be like and you don't tell her, what do you think will happen when she comes to work for your company? Or let's say you have a sales opening and you tell the applicant that you have salespeople who earn $100,000 a year and that there is no reason he can't be at this level, too. What you don't tell him is that there are just two salespeople at this income level and they are the owner's sons and have been given all the large accounts. In actuality, the average salesperson earns about a quarter of this after the first year and is lucky to even make a living for the first six months.

In their eagerness to fill a vacancy, managers often oversell the job and company. It is easy to find yourself saying things like, "This is a great company to work for," or "You'll really like it here." The anxious applicant wants to believe this, and when someone is hungry, everything looks appetizing. Once hired, though, reality sets in. There is nothing wrong with praising your company, but when you are making the job and company appealing to an applicant, stick to the facts. Describe a typical workday, and be sure to describe the company culture the way it really is. New employees are quick to figure out when they have been misled about the job and may quit as a result.

Deal with firing guidelines during the interview. Managers spend a great deal of time telling applicants what qualities and abilities are needed but neglect to outline what is not acceptable. In addition to explaining what qualities you are seeking, tell the applicant what the company won't tolerate. Be honest about the downside, even though you may find it painful to do so.

Promises made during job interviews can lead to litigation later. There have been lawsuits brought by fired employees who believed they were misled about conditions at a company before they accepted a position there. From both a moral and a legal standpoint, it is best not to exaggerate opportunities or conditions at the company during interviews with prospective employees.

Speeding Up
Reference Checking

MOST HIRING MANAGERS AND SPECIALISTS take on the full burden of contacting the applicant's references. This is not necessary. Why not have the candidate assist you in the reference-checking process? If the candidate is interested in the position—and has nothing to hide—he or she will be happy to provide the assistance you need to verify that the information about his or her work history is correct.

Provide the candidate with the references you determined during the interview that you would most like to speak with. Have the candidate contact these individuals and ask them to speak freely with you. The candidate should ask the references to call you or arrange a time for you to call them. If a reference does not feel comfortable talking about the candidate at work because of the company's policy on providing references, have the candidate set up a time when the reference can be contacted at home.

In short, have the candidate make all the arrangements for you to speak with the references so that you don't waste your valuable time chasing people down. We also suggest having the candidate send his résumé to all the references so that you can ask them whether it is correct (a powerful move on your part).

COLLABORATION WITH MUTUAL GAIN

There is a simple reason why the new system will work for everyone concerned. Getting a new employee or a new job should be a win-win scenario. The company gets a good employee; the employee gets a good job. The hiring process is a way to meet both these needs. Both parties stand to gain, and both parties are winners.

Let's look at this new system of checking references from the standpoint of what's in and what's out.

What's In:

1. You choose the references you feel will provide the best information about the applicant.
2. The applicant contacts these references and arranges a convenient time for you to speak with them.
3. You get the information you want from the reference and clear up any concerns you may have.
4. You remain in complete control of the hiring process, including the reference-checking phase.

What's Out:

1. The candidate provides you with the names of the references he or she would like contacted.
2. You play telephone tag with the references the applicant has given you.
3. The reference tells you what the candidate wants you to hear, and you accept it and do not probe any further.

4. The candidate keeps indirect control of the references you can speak with.

So what are your options? You can take the position that it is just too difficult to check someone's references and forget about doing it altogether. You can do it the old way, trying to track down the references yourself and then hoping they'll speak with you. Or you can try the new way, as many have, and enjoy the tremendous results it produces. It is a system designed to help the good candidate, not a way to protect those who don't want their work record checked. It is time for win-win thinking regarding the employment process.

IT REALLY WORKS

Does using the candidate as your helper work? Let us share two of the many stories that have been related to us.

A hiring manager explained that his company was serious about a particular candidate under consideration for a key position. When that candidate asked how soon he could start, he was told that his references had to be checked first. The candidate volunteered, "If you would like, I can get hold of these people for you and have them call." Within three hours, all the references had called and the reference-checking process was completed. This manager commented that it never occurred to him to have the candidate contact the references, but he was going to make this practice a permanent part of his employment system.

A woman told us in one of our seminars that with her current employer it took almost three weeks for the company to complete the reference checking on her. In fact, after the first week she had called to make sure that she was still in the running for the position and was assured that she certainly was. They were just waiting for her reference check to be completed. At the time, she had thought to herself that maybe she should offer to contact the references and ask them to call the employer. However, she decided this would not be appropriate, since the person doing the reference checking might be offended and think she was indicating that he wasn't doing his job. She now sees that it would have been a sensible thing to do.

Now we know you're probably thinking, "What about the person who goes to his three or four best friends and sets them up to be the people they want you to speak with?" His friend Joe becomes the president of the company, Karen becomes his immediate supervisor, Barry becomes a peer, and Dave becomes his subordinate.

To begin with, we cannot imagine this scheme being pulled off successfully. If an astute reference checker uses unexpected and thorough questioning techniques (which are explored in Part V), this could never happen. Good questioning will immediately stop this farce dead in its tracks. And if you have any doubt, you can always call the reference back to verify that it was the person to whom you thought you were speaking. If this still bothers you, then have the candidate arrange a convenient (and exact) time for you to contact the reference.

Whichever situation you choose, there is no reason that you should spend your valuable time chasing down references when the candidate will gladly do it for you. Why should you care how the reference contact is made so long as you get to talk with the person?

We have had hiring managers and human resources staff members tell us that this system has made the task of checking references immeasurably easier and quicker. It has made their jobs more enjoyable and their hiring process more effective. We have spoken to job seekers and recommended that they use this new system to their advantage as job candidates. We advise them that when they learn they are truly in the running for a position, they should immediately ask whether their references will be checked. If so, they should offer to help contact the references to ease the burden on the employer and to speed up the process so they can go to work as soon as possible. It is a proactive approach that can help them to be viewed as stronger and more viable candidates. Remember this yourself if you are ever on the other side of the desk as an applicant.

Having the candidates help you contact their references is an obvious way to facilitate the reference-checking process. It works because it puts everyone in a win-win situation. The candidate is able to start the new position quickly, and you have completed your employment duties in a timely manner. A strong candidate, with nothing to hide, will more than welcome the opportunity to assist you because it will be in his or her favor. Whereas poor candidates, who want everything they say to be accepted without question, do not like it—because it's almost guaranteed to expose them. If someone is too lazy to perform this task, you might well ask yourself: Will he or she be similarly lazy on the job?

THE OVERALL ADVANTAGES

There are five definite advantages to using this new system:

1. By having the applicant ask a reference to speak with you, that person now becomes a personal reference. As you will see in Part V, this is the only real way you will get consistent, in-depth reference information about your candidate.

2. It solves the legal question of obtaining a release from the candidate before asking people to disclose personal information about him or her.
3. The applicant does the initial contact work for you. You don't waste your valuable time playing telephone tag, and then pleading with someone to give you information.
4. It greatly speeds up the hiring process, possibly preventing the loss of a good candidate.
5. The applicant will view you as someone who is in control of the situation, and your company as one that is thorough and selective in choosing new employees. This will make the candidate feel good about coming to work there.

ADVICE FOR THE JOB CANDIDATE

Although reference checks may be beyond your control, you can manage what is being said about you by choosing your references wisely, keeping them informed about your employment situation, and briefing them prior to receiving any telephone calls.

Select your references in advance of the interview. Choose people who are knowledgeable about your abilities and performance. This means current or former managers, peers, subordinates, and clients. Identify those who you think will make positive observations and comments about your work history and accomplishments.

Once you understand the company and its requirements, offer the names of appropriate references who can help you to obtain the new position. References are a great asset to obtaining a new job, so use them wisely. Your references should be able to properly comment about your work. If the potential position involves customer contact or sales, past customers and suppliers may also be useful as references.

Try to select people with good communication skills who can and will converse with someone about you. People who are hard to reach, unclear, or evasive may hurt your efforts. Provide their full names, where they are employed, the position they hold, and both their work and home telephone numbers.

Advise your references that they can expect to be called about you. Try to find out the name of the person who will be calling and give this information to your references. It is best to keep your references informed about the progress of your job search. Provide them with copies of your résumé, and tell them how your interview went. By doing this they will be better prepared to tailor their remarks to best support you. If someone is hesitant about being your reference or does not seem to understand what is needed, replace that person with a more suitable reference.

Most companies will give little or no information regarding current or past employees. If your current or past employer prohibits its managers or others from providing references, contact former managers, coworkers, and subordinates who have joined other companies or who have retired and ask them whether they would be willing to be a reference and provide a recommendation for you. Also, if you are currently employed and want your search to remain confidential, you will need to contact people from earlier employers who knew you and ask them to be a reference for you.

In fact, we go so far as to recommend that, as a candidate, you ask all potential employers whether they will provide a reference on your performance with their company in the event that you leave or are released. Advise a new employer that you intend to work hard to be a top performer and expect that this information (or whatever report the company has about you) will be relayed, if requested, to a potential employer. If the hiring officer says that the company won't say anything good (or bad) about you, you may want to consider a more progressive company that won't just file away those important years of your personal life and career.

If you have had a negative or poor relationship with a former company or manager, you want to address this situation during the interview. It is best to be honest and straightforward in explaining a situation or period of employment that just did not work out. By doing so, you may be able to turn a negative situation into a positive opportunity.

Remember that prospective employers will want to ask questions and clarify any concerns that they have. Often what isn't said is more important than what is said. Encourage your references to be open and honest about their past association with you. You can anticipate that questions will be asked regarding your strengths and weaknesses. The areas that will probably be explored are your communication skills, ability to get along with others, adaptability, reaction to pressure, and ability to do your work. Most successful companies will check your references. If discrepancies or problems exist, you may be eliminated from consideration for employment.

Your references are part of your employment search. Maintain and cultivate these relationships. It is best to develop references throughout your career so that when you need them, they will be available. You need to have references who are knowledgeable, prepared, and enthusiastic. A good reference will dramatically improve your chances of landing a new job.

Part III Summary

In Part III, you discovered that:

⸱ When told that their past record and performance will be checked, most job candidates immediately see the need for being truthful.

⸱ To keep the applicant honest, control must be maintained during the interviewing process. The person doing the interviewing needs to continually probe and ask questions to fully understand what the candidate is saying.

⸱ You should be honest with the applicant during the interview. Do not oversell the job or company. Let the applicant know exactly what will be expected of him or her if hired.

⸱ During the interview, it is important to identify the names of key people in the applicant's work life who can provide you with a good perspective of how that person performed in previous jobs.

⸱ There is a new system of using the candidate to contact references, which speeds up the process. The candidate who really wants the job will do anything, within reason, to assist in the hiring process.

Searching Public Records

Why Public Records Searches Are Necessary

BECAUSE EMPLOYERS ARE INCREASINGLY BEING held liable when an employee with a clear history of criminal activity commits a crime of the same nature during the course of his or her employment, companies need to protect themselves by exercising reasonable care when selecting new employees. This may include conducting a criminal records check on all final candidates, a credit check if the applicant will be working in a financial area, and a driving record check if the applicant will be operating a company vehicle. Employers in sensitive industries may also want to perform an identity check on an applicant.

Credentials and document verification for criminal convictions, workers compensation awards, credit standing, educational attainment, and driving violations are lawful if done properly. There are several simple rules employers need to follow before implementing these checks to ensure that they are not exposed to potential legal liability or other problems. This is where help from an outside service firm can save a great deal of time and trouble.

CRIMINAL RECORDS CHECKS

The U.S. Supreme Court determined in a 1976 court case that the use of criminal records does not violate an individual's constitutional right of privacy. Most states have allowed for criminal records to be made available, but have developed laws regarding the use of criminal records in making employment decisions so that no one is unfairly discriminated against because of prior convictions. These laws vary from state to state. If your company inquires about convictions on its job application form, it should be clearly stated that a criminal conviction *will not* automatically disqualify the applicant from employment.

To ensure a thorough and accurate criminal record search, information must be obtained directly from the court of origin where cases are processed in a given jurisdiction. This simply means that every county where an applicant has lived or worked must be searched. The specific courts to be searched are determined from the applicant's past residence, plus educational and employment history. This information should be provided by the applicant on the application form and can also be obtained from information developed during the screening process. To conduct a more thorough search you may also want to check the state police records in all states where the applicant has been educated or employed. Having a date of birth is an extremely helpful piece of information and can be used as an identifier in the case of similar names.

Violations of federal laws are processed through federal courts, while violations of state laws are processed through county and city courts. There are no state courts that adjudicate (initiate, resolve, and file) criminal cases. The majority of states have central repositories for collecting criminal information, but this information is not always accessible to the public, nor do the repositories always contain all the necessary information. A state's city and county courts, along with law enforcement officials, are asked to provide their records to the central state repository; however, the repository does not have the enforcement power to ensure that this is done. Criminal records provided by the state cannot be relied upon exclusively to determine whether an individual has a history of criminal activity because not all information may have been reported.

In some states, it can take up to three months to obtain the results of a criminal search. A number of state repositories require the submission of a signed and notarized authorization form from the individual whose name is being searched. Some require fingerprinting before a search can be conducted.

There are a number of firms that specialize in providing criminal checks for client companies. These firms have people in every state who literally go into a county courthouse or have access to a county's database to investigate a person's background. The turnaround time usually runs from three to five days.

Several independent companies now offer third-party databases for criminal records searches. However, these databases may not be completely reliable. A number of courts are not automated and information from these courts may not be included. Also, the time span of information available through them is often limited to recent years. These databases are only as good as the information they are able to gather.

In summary, it behooves the employer to obtain as much information as possible from the candidate, and to go forward from there (see Exhibit 11-1). Of course, the presence of criminal activity should not result in the automatic rejection of someone. There may be mitigating or extenuating conditions such as the nature and seriousness of the crime; the circumstances under which it oc-

Exhibit 11-1. Hot tips.

When an applicant admits to a criminal offense, always obtain the following information:

1. Date of occurrence—which can include arrest date, court date, and/or conviction date
2. Location—the specific court, including city, county, and state
3. The nature of the case(s), including the level of offense (felony, misdemeanor, etc.)

Criminal records cannot be researched only by name. Alternative identification is also required, such as social security number and, more important, date of birth.

curred; how long ago the crime was committed; the age of the person at the time of the crime; the social and developmental history of the perpetrator; whether the crime was an isolated event; and most important, evidence of the individual's rehabilitation.

There are no hard-and-fast rules to follow in evaluating someone with a criminal record. Automatic disqualification is harsh and inhumane. Each case must be examined on its own merits and a decision rendered by the hiring authority.

WORKERS COMPENSATION RECORDS

The Americans with Disabilities Act (ADA) prohibits an employer from asking an applicant prior to an offer of employment whether he or she is disabled and the extent of the disability or about any workers compensation claims. Thus, the prudent course of action is to make the job offer contingent on the applicant passing a physical examination or medical screen, which then could involve a check on the applicant's medical and workers compensation history.

Workers compensation records can be a useful screening tool, particularly in physically demanding positions. This information will help you to verify employment history, screen out applicants who have a history of fraudulent claims, screen out individuals who could pose a health or safety threat to themselves or others, and provide information to state officials who regulate workers compensation and second-injury funds.

CREDIT REPORTS

Inquiries about financial status and credit rating should be limited to situations where there is a clear business necessity for the check. The company's finance department can normally conduct a credit check. Credit checks are conducted routinely when granting credit to customers. This is a touchy area covered by the Fair Credit Reporting Act (FCRA), which is explained fully later in this chapter.

EDUCATIONAL ATTAINMENT

We strongly recommend that any educational claims be verified, even if the degree received is not required for the position. Falsification and exaggeration of a person's education is rising at an alarming rate.

Most high school and college registrars will verify attendance and/or degrees by telephone. Some schools require that a faxed written request be sent along with a signed release from the candidate. Others may charge a small fee for this information.

When checking on a degree from a college or university, the information required would be the applicant's social security number and his or her name at the time of attendance. To verify a high school diploma, you will need the applicant's date of birth and the name used when she attended. In either case, it always helps researchers when you know the date of graduation. Often, records are archived and this helps them to determine where they will be able to find this information. To verify an applicant's G.E.D., contact the state board of education. Keep a record of the results of the telephone calls. If you are ever in doubt, you can always ask the candidate to provide you with an original graduation certificate or diploma with an official seal.

We also recommend that you make sure that the school is an accredited school. There has been a resurgence of nonaccredited schools boasting of degrees for sale.

DRIVING RECORDS

When operating company vehicles or equipment is an important or essential part of an employee's job, the employer has a legitimate interest in the applicant's driving record. An employee who operates a motor vehicle on behalf of the employer can be a serious liability. The ADA authorizes such inquiries only when driving is an essential function of the job. Exhibit 11-2 illustrates a separate form for this purpose.

A driving record check can also be a valuable source of information about the candidate. If someone has a suspended or revoked license, you need to find out how he or she will get back and forth to work. If there are repeated offenses or DWI violations, this may cause future performance problems. The applicant's driving history provides valuable insight into that person's character and

Exhibit 11-2. Driving information form.

Driving information: The position for which you are applying requires driving a company vehicle and/or the company providing insurance. Please complete the following. Your application will not be processed if not filled out completely.

Do you have a valid driver's license?   Yes   ☐ No

If yes, please give your license number _____

State _____   Expiration Date _____

Have your driving privileges ever been revoked or suspended?
☐ Yes   ☐ No   If yes, please explain.

_____

_____

_____

Have you been involved in a traffic accident in the past three years?
☐ Yes   ☐ No   If yes, please explain.

_____

_____

_____

List the number and nature of moving traffic violations of which you have been convicted in the past three years.

_____

_____

_____

_____

_____

reliability. Also, the report can be used to verify the driver's address and date of birth.

Driving record information is available from individual state motor vehicle departments. There is no national database. Under the federally mandated Commercial Driver's License System (CDL), drivers may no longer carry licenses from more than one state. Legally, all commercial license information is maintained by the driver's home state.

The official driving record is usually called an abstract. It contains a wealth of information about the licensee. The presence or absence of violations, accidents, and points speaks volumes about the person holding the license.

LICENSING BOARDS

Verifying that someone is a licensed CPA, attorney, teacher, or health-care professional is a fairly easy task and can usually be confirmed over the phone. There is an association for each of these professions that maintains records within each state. The information required would be name and social security number. In some cases these associations may verify the current address or date of birth in order to avoid any errors. They will also let you know if this person is in good standing or if there have ever been any violations or complaints filed against him or her.

SCREENING DIRECTORY

The Guide to Background Investigations is an excellent source directory for employers and others involved in background investigations and can be used as a tool to help access information contained in public records. First published in 1987 with the title *National Employment Screening Directory*, the information is updated extensively every two years. New listings include U.S. Federal Appellate Courts, Canadian Schools, and a source for Canadian Criminal Records.

The guide contains four major sections: State Records Directory, Locator Directory, Federal Records Directory, and Educational Records Directory.

The State Records Directory is arranged alphabetically by state. For each state, a brief introduction provides an overview of access to the state's records and includes the state's hot-line number for additional assistance. This section includes contacts for obtaining corporation commission information, criminal records, driving and vehicle records, license verification through state boards, vital statistics (birth, death, marriage and divorce), and workers compensation records. Listings detail procedures, fees, and additional notes on accessing state records. Within the State Records Directory, courthouses are listed state by state for access to criminal, misdemeanor, and civil records that are stored at the county level.

Each state section ends with a city-county cross-reference, a state map, and a map index. When only an individual's address is known, then the cross-reference, map, and index can be used to determine the county of residence as well as surrounding counties. The Locator Directory provides a zip code, state, and county cross-reference that can be used to verify the county in which an address is located. This cross-reference table is helpful for cities that may overlap more than one county.

The Federal Records Directory begins with a brief description of the federal court system and how it can be used to access civil, criminal, and bankruptcy cases. Listed by state, entries include the address, telephone number, and procedures for each district and bankruptcy court.

The Educational Records Directory lists over four thousand accredited colleges, universities, and trade and technical schools. Listed alphabetically, each entry supplies the address and telephone number for the registrar's office, along with the policy and procedures for accessing information. Schools are also cross-referenced by state and city.

The new Canadian Records Directory includes sources for Canadian driving records, Canadian criminal records, and Canadian postsecondary education verifications. Canadian school listings include contact information for 235 Canadian postsecondary educational institutions. Contact information is also provided for the registrar's office of each school.

The Guide to Background Investigations is a public records directory book in a single publication. The broad scope of the book combined with the depth and detail of its listings makes it an excellent resource for researchers and investigators looking for background information. It provides companies with basically all of the contact information necessary to perform their own in-house investigations for a variety of background searches. The guide can be purchased by calling 800-247-8713 and is also available on CD-ROM. For companies that do not want to purchase the book, this information is also accessible on the Web, through your local library, or in other directories.

Courts.net has developed a Web site that provides access and information to Web sites maintained by courts nationwide. There is also a site for federal courts, which includes supreme courts, circuit courts, district courts, bankruptcy courts, and tax courts. Many state and county courts also have Web sites that will provide you with contact information.

There are Web sites that can furnish a driving record of an individual for a fee. Driving history will vary by each state but typically includes personal identifiers; driving status; license type; and driving restrictions or infractions, if any are on file.

Colleges and universities generally have a Web site, and a few of them offer the option of verifying a person's degree online. The National Student Clearinghouse (www.studentclearinghouse.com) and Credentials Inc. (www.degreecheck.com) provide student verification for many accredited universities within the United States.

When using a company on the Web, a fee is usually charged for the information, which can sometimes be quite costly depending on the amount of information sought. An outside investigative service can also be used to compile the desired information and is often more cost-effective.

Understanding the Fair Credit Reporting Act

The Fair Credit Reporting Act (FCRA), 15 U.S.C. § 1681 *et seq.*, as amended by the Consumer Credit Reporting Reform Act of 1996 (CCRRA), as further amended by the Consumer Reporting Employment Clarification Act of 1998 (CRECA), applies to background checks if an outside service is employed to conduct the investigation. If an employer chooses to investigate an applicant's background using employees within the company, the FCRA does not apply. However, many companies do not have the time or resources necessary to conduct a thorough investigation and therefore employ the services of an outside search firm, which imposes some extra requirements.

Before a consumer report may be obtained from an outside firm or consumer-reporting agency, the employer must provide the applicant or employee with a clear and conspicuous disclosure (in a document that consists solely of the disclosure) that a consumer report may be obtained for employment purposes and obtain written authorization from the applicant or employee. The authorization for release form discussed in Chapter 8 (see Exhibit 8-2) fulfills this requirement.

If an employer does not hire the candidate as a result of information obtained in a consumer report, the employer must advise the applicant of the intent to take such action, provide the applicant with a copy of the report, and also supply a summary of his or her rights as prepared by the Federal Trade Commission. In addition, the employer should notify the applicant of his or her right to dispute the report directly to the reporting agency, explain that the agency did not make the adverse decision, and provide the agency's name and contact number. Consult Chapter 16 for further discussion on handling the rejected applicant.

There is one additional administrative requirement under the FCRA with which the employer must comply. A certification must be made to the consumer-reporting agency supplying the information that all the requirements and steps of the FCRA have been taken and are being followed (see Exhibit 11-3).

In summary, the FCRA is designed to promote the accuracy, fairness, and privacy of information about an applicant supplied by credit bureaus, public record sources, and others. Employers, however, who show that the information on a credit or investigative report turns out to be false are not obligated to hire previous applicants.

Exhibit 11-3. Request for background reports.

(Company Identification)

TO: [*Consumer-Reporting Agency*]

ᖽ As required by the Fair Credit Reporting Act, [*your company name*] certifies that it has complied and will comply with the disclosure and adverse action requirement of the FCRA.

ᖽ We have made a clear and conspicuous disclosure to the applicant, in a document solely for that purpose, that a consumer report may be obtained, which has been signed by the individual.

ᖽ The information obtained will not be used in violation of any federal or state equal opportunity law or regulation, and if any adverse action is taken based on the consumer report, a copy of the report and a summary of the applicant's rights will be provided to the individual, as well as advising how the information may be disputed.

Signature: _____
(Authorized Representative)

Printed Name: _____

Title: _____

Date: _____

Spotting Criminals
and Troublemakers

AFTER THE TERRORIST ATTACKS IN New York City and Washington, D.C., on September 11, 2001, there is clearly an increased need to prevent the wrong people from being hired or used by businesses and other organizations. Companies want an extra level of comfort in knowing whom they are hiring and working with.

Many companies are now conducting criminal records checks on candidates whom they hire, and the number is increasing daily. Most of these companies are using firms that specialize in criminal checks, because it is a time-consuming task that can produce questionable results.

Since each state and county has different levels and methods of recording background information, the results can vary. For example, someone might be charged with a crime, but there may not be an indication of how the case ended. Often pardons or expunged reports might not show up correctly. If someone, who was involved in a drug case, received amnesty for providing information that assisted authorities, chances are this will be considered a closed case and no information will be given out to the public. In a rural court, the information may be stored in a cardboard box in the basement and not be readily available. The whole process is time consuming and not very effective.

Unfortunately, it is difficult to use or rely on such an inconsistent system to spot candidates with a history of undesirable behavior, and therefore to prevent bringing them into the organization. Under current law, the federal databases, which are usually very thorough and reliable, are not available for employment purposes.

It may sound like we are implying that criminal records should not be sought on an individual you are thinking of hiring, but that is not the case. We merely want to point out that the current system for retrieving information is not 100 percent accurate.

HOW THE SYSTEM FAILS US

There are two federal systems for identifying people with a criminal record or history of mental illness or domestic abuse. The National Criminal Information Center (NCIC) has been available for years to state and local police departments to identify criminal behavior and dangerous personality problems. The National Instant Check System (NICS) was begun on November 30, 1998, to conduct quick background checks on anyone who wanted to buy a handgun from a licensed dealer. In both systems a person's name, address, and social security number (SSN) are run through a series of computer databases that hold the names of millions of people. Included are convicted felons, fugitives, the mentally ill, drug users, illegal aliens, domestic abusers, people with protective orders against them, and those dishonorably discharged from the military. The information is almost instantaneous or available in a couple of hours. These systems, paid for by U.S. tax-payers, are state-of-the-art methods for conducting back-ground checks. However, it is illegal to use them for employment purposes, except by government agencies.

We do know that some companies have found a way to tap into these extensive databases. Using their civic contacts, or their security units usually made up of former police officers or police officers working part-time for them, they run the names of prospective new hires through the system to see what happens. It is not the legal way to perform a criminal check for employment, but we know that it is being done.

It merely provides an employer with the necessary information to avoid a serious hiring mistake. We are hoping that the day will come soon when employers can legally check applicants against the State Department's terrorist watch list, immigration service records, or the national criminal database. Every company has a legiti-mate right to know as much as possible about the people it is hiring, and the system currently in place does not allow this to happen.

Many of us in the background-screening field want a federal statute ensuring access to computerized federal criminal records containing conviction data. We firmly recommend that legislation be brought forth that would provide timely access to centralized databases containing criminal records. The lack of access to national criminal data means background checks may fail to detect all crim-inal records, because checks done in one state do not nec-essarily reveal information on convictions in another state. Under the current methods, there is no guarantee that the people you hire are free of criminal offenses or are not on terrorist watch lists. It is possible you could employ someone with a criminal history and not know it.

THE IDENTITY PROBLEM

An identity check is a new element in the background-checking arsenal. Basic identity verification shows that a person's name, address, and SSN all match up. It is ensuring that the person you are hiring is who he represents himself to be. It is a well-known fact that someone can purchase another identity for a few hundred dollars, which includes a driver's license, social security card, and other identification.

It is difficult for employers to detect any wrongdoing when someone has skillfully prepared documentation. It almost takes special training to know what to look for. But, suffice it to say, this aspect should be in the mind of all hiring authorities. In many ways, an identity check is probably just as important as a criminal background check in that it tries to spot the undesirable and certainly unwanted person. A senior law enforcement official told us that the number of individuals using someone else's identity has reached alarming proportions in the United States and throughout the world. If someone thinks his identity has been stolen, he should immediately notify the three credit-reporting agencies listed in Appendix B.

The root of the identity theft problem is the lack of a formal, centralized identification system. Also, authorities do not always verify the true identity of the person to whom they issue a document. And, counterfeit ID cards have become more difficult to detect. Proposals now abound calling for retina scans, fingerprinting, and a national ID card.

EMPLOYMENT ELIGIBILITY VERIFICATION

By law, employers are required to verify every employee within three days of hire by completing an Employment

Verification Form, more commonly known as the I-9, and by obtaining two forms of proof of the person's identity. The form can only be completed after proper identification has been produced. Identification can be submitted in the form of a passport, driver's license, social security card, birth certificate, U.S. military card, or alien registration card. The company must also keep a copy of the identification supplied by the applicant in its files.

Although it is not necessary to complete the I-9 form until the applicant has been hired, it is an excellent tool to use as part of the preemployment process. In order to complete this required form, the employer needs to see proper identification from the applicant. If the candidate refuses or cannot produce the proper identification, there is no reason to consider him or her for employment.

ILLEGAL IMMIGRANTS

Illegal immigrants, many armed with phony social security and permanent resident green cards, have integrated themselves into the U.S. mainstream by taking low-wage jobs that employers can't fill with the native workforce. An estimated seven to ten million undocumented immigrants live in the United States. Experts say that Mexicans make up about 60 percent of the undocumented population, and Central Americans account for about a fifth of the total.

A major problem in this regard is with employers who hire undocumented workers so that they can pay them cash and avoid paying for workers compensation insurance, unemployment benefits, and overtime, which would come with legitimate employment. The Immigration and Nationality Act requires that any employer who wants to use foreign temporary workers must certify that there are insufficient available and qualified Americans to do the work.

Employers are supposed to be on the front lines of curtailing undocumented workers. The Immigration Reform Act of 1986, which gave amnesty to approximately three million undocumented immigrants, required employers to make employees present documents proving their eligibility to work in this country. Employers who do not comply with the law face civil and criminal penalties if the U.S. Immigration and Naturalization Service (INS) audits the company's payroll. The INS has taken action against a number of companies and is committed to enforcing compliance with immigration laws and protecting America's workforce.

A recent analysis estimated that almost half of the country's farm workers are undocumented, roughly a quarter of the people working in private households are illegal immigrants, as are about 10 percent of restaurant employees. Also, about 6 percent of those in construction and manufacturing are undocumented. Obviously, illegal immigrants have become a major factor in the U.S. workforce.

SOCIAL SECURITY NUMBERS

A major problem exists today in using an SSN as an identifier. The fact that all nineteen of the September 11, 2001, hijackers had SSNs including several that were stolen, has cast a spotlight on the role SSNs play in identity theft. In fact, the terrorists had several SSNs in their possession as well as several identities. Thirteen of the hijackers did not steal their SSNs but obtained them legally.

A false SSN is clearly a useful tool for obtaining new employment and other purposes. These numbers, which were originally intended only as a way for the government to track earnings and benefits, are now used widely as a personal identifier for obtaining employment, credit, and medical services, as well as many other reasons. SSN verification is still the best method for ensuring that the person is, indeed, the person he or she purports to be.

Conducting an SSN verification is accomplished primarily through the utilization of credit bureaus, such as TransUnion, Equifax, and Experian (see Appendix B). The service provides information regarding the results of its investigation, which includes the state and year of issue of the SSN, address of the SSN user, employers of the user, the year of the user's birth, and additional or multiple users of the number.

If the information received does not match what the applicant provided, the employer should question the person about these findings. The difference or omission of information may be explained. It is also possible that the applicant is the victim of someone using his or her SSN for dubious purposes. However, there is no legal reason to change one's SSN. If a person has more than one number, there is probably something serious going on.

CONTACTING POLICE AUTHORITIES

There are an increasing number of job applicants presenting phony identification and documentation. There are now many sources for obtaining false identification and documentation from phony birth certificates to college diplomas. There is even software to make fake documents at home. Everyone needs to be alert to such fraud, and to participate in trying to stop it.

It is illegal to use, possess, or manufacture fake or counterfeit documents. Law enforcement agencies at all levels of government are working to spot and dismantle counterfeiting operations. Anyone who encounters counterfeiting should immediately contact the local police. They will notify the appropriate local, state, or federal agency. The cooperation of everyone, including those in business and other organizations, is essential in combating this insidious illegal activity.

Part IV Summary

In Part IV, you discovered that:

ꙮ Employers are being held liable for employees' actions while on the job.

ꙮ Employers can protect themselves from a negligent hiring lawsuit by conducting background checks on applicants.

ꙮ The Fair Credit Reporting Act has specific guidelines that must be followed when a third party is used to provide information about a candidate.

ꙮ Identity theft has become a serious problem. Basic identity verification will show that a person's name, address, and social security number match up.

ꙮ Based on the information provided by the reference on the job application, an employer can only check the states or counties listed. Employers do not have access to federal systems that would provide a clear criminal history on an individual.

Techniques That Work

Effective Reference Checking

YOU WON'T BE EFFECTIVE AT checking references unless you see the benefits of doing it. All the techniques covered in this chapter won't make you effective in this function unless you believe you are doing something necessary and positive for your company, as well as for the candidate. No one gains from a hiring mismatch. In particular, the reputations of those who hire someone who is not qualified for the position may be affected.

Unfortunately, most people assigned to checking references do not like doing it, and it is difficult to be good at something you do not enjoy doing. The real basis for success in checking references is a positive feeling about the task on the part of the person doing the checking. If you are confident in your ability to ask the right questions, your attitude and enthusiasm will rub off on the people you are talking with—and you will acquire the information you need.

TYPES OF CHECKING

There are two types of background checks: records checks and reference checks.

Records Check

Secretaries or clerical personnel can perform a records check to determine whether the information the applicant has supplied on his or her résumé or application is accurate. This check is nothing more than determining honesty and confirming that the previous dates of employment, job titles, academic degrees, professional licenses, and such are correct. Unfortunately, this is as far as many companies go in their checking. They may call it reference checking, but that would be a misnomer.

Reference Check

The reference check is usually carried out by the hiring manager or employment staff and determines actual competency on the job. This type of check involves an in-depth conversation with someone who knows or has worked with the candidate. Depending on the depth of your conversation, you can explore one, two, or three of the following personal conduct areas:

1. *Sociability*. How well does the candidate get along with and relate to other people? Information on this issue is fairly easy to discover and discuss, and can usually be obtained from anyone you speak with—both personal and professional references.

2. *Work habits and ability*. How well did this person perform in his or her previous positions? Obviously, this information must come from people who worked with the person, such as fellow employees, peers, subordinates, supervisors, or company officials. You want to assess the person's technical or functional ability, and also attitude on the job.

3. *Personal character*. What is the candidate's basic personality, including morals and ethics? This level of in-

formation may be desired for a key or very sensitive position and will have to come from talking not only with work associates but also with close friends. It may move beyond normal reference checking into a private investigation or a background investigation for a security clearance.

Based on a survey of seventy-two major companies in the Midwest, together with responses to questions on the subject of the depth of background checking of job applicants raised at seminars, we found that 58 percent of companies conducted both records and reference checks (see Exhibit 13-1).

THE BENEFITS OF REFERENCE CHECKING

Let's look at the positive aspects of checking references:

1. *Reference checking provides clear testimonials to support your decision to hire a particular person.* You'll feel much better about your hiring decision if the references speak favorably about the candidate.

2. *The reference check may provide additional evidence of accomplishments or reveal factors that were not covered in the interview.* When we perform a reference check on someone, we hear favorable comments that reflect well on the applicant but were not brought out during the interview. The references will often make comments like he is a good family man, she is very religious, he does not smoke or drink, she is not a substance abuser, he runs three miles every day, and so on.

3. *It provides good management-development advice that enables you to best fit the person into your organization.* The more you know about someone in advance, the better you will be able to help him or her to succeed in your company. What you learn up front is only what you will find

Exhibit 13-1. Depth of checking undertaken.

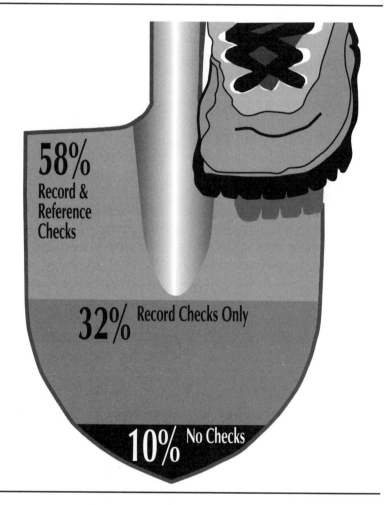

58%
Record &
Reference
Checks

32% Record Checks Only

10% No Checks

out three months, six months, or a year or so after he or she has been working for you. Isn't it better to discover the information sooner rather than later and proactively address the situation, not just to react later on?

Everyone has flat spots, and if you do a good job checking references, you will discover them. It has often been said that our greatest strengths are also our greatest weaknesses. For example, if someone is very aggressive, you will need to determine whether this type of personality fits well in your organization. If someone puts in a lot of hours on the job and is being considered for a supervisory or management position, you will need to look at how well she works with others and her ability to delegate.

4. *Effective reference checking establishes you as someone who can protect your company from a poor hiring decision.* A company invests a considerable amount of time, money, and energy in hiring and training a new employee. If the new person doesn't work out, for whatever reason, the costs skyrocket. An employee who fails and leaves after a few months can cost a company anywhere from $5,000 for an hourly worker to $75,000 for a manager in lost productivity and money spent on training, to say nothing of lowered morale and profits. If you can sit in front of a hiring manager and present solid facts and opinions to support the hiring decision, you will be viewed as a valuable member of the company.

5. *It gives justice where justice is due.* In other words, you'll hear good things about good people and poor things about marginal performers. Good people are penalized when we do not hear what others have to say about them.

Checking someone's references is well worth the effort. A few questions to the right people will help to weed out the candidate who handles interviews well but performs poorly on the job. It will also highlight good employees who are not adept at interviewing. We suggest that if you are not able to get references on a candidate, look for someone else.

EXCHANGING INFORMATION

There are very effective and workable methods for getting people to speak with you about someone they know. In fact, they are so obvious that you might even say they are not really techniques. Yet, we assure you, most people trying to check references do not realize these techniques exist, let alone use them. However, before we discuss exactly what these techniques are, let's look at how information is exchanged.

Information flows in a predictable way and is exchanged back and forth on two levels, formally and informally. There is virtually no way that information on the informal level can be controlled, whereas gathering information on the formal level is usually a complicated and tedious task.

One friend talking to another about someone they both know is an example of the informal method, as is a manager talking to another manager about a current or former employee, or one employee telling another employee what he or she thinks about someone with whom they both work. It is two people talking about a third person, which is a perfectly normal occurrence. In fact, informal conversation makes up a good part of our daily lives.

The formal method requires that you get an official statement from a company or person. This is a difficult task because the right officer must be involved and this process takes a lot of time and patience.

On the formal level, a limited amount of information is exchanged, whereas at the informal level, there is an unrestricted flow of information. The primary difference in business is that the formal method functions in keeping with a rigid company policy where the personnel department verifies only dates, job titles, and rates of pay. By contrast, the informal method circumvents that policy by allowing you to speak with former supervisors, peers, and subordinates, who are the best sources of information about an applicant's past job performance.

Let's look at how this works in an employment situation. If you call supervisor John Doe at XYZ Company and ask him about someone who used to work for him, chances are he won't tell you very much because he has to follow his company's policy on not releasing such information and will refer you to human resources (HR). But if the candidate gives the same supervisor, John Doe, as his personal reference, and you call and advise Mr. Doe that he has been given as a personal reference by the applicant, chances are he will see the situation in an entirely different light and cooperate fully with you.

Under the formal method, you get little or no information because of legal or other fears, such as possibly giving the wrong information or not representing the company properly. With the informal method, you will usually get natural and insightful comments and observations that can be quite valuable in your hiring decision. Obviously, of the two roads to travel, the informal path is most likely to get you where you want to go and will get you there much faster.

The formal road is painfully slow to travel because it involves one company trying to talk to another company, which is impossible. You don't call companies—you call people. The informal road is easier to traverse because it involves one person talking with another person (see Exhibit 13-2). To be a good reference checker, you must be willing to take the so-called open road.

Then why do we find it so terrifying to speak with others about someone we are thinking of hiring? When you stop to think about it, checking references is a very natural thing that we all do at times, and not only when we are thinking of hiring someone. We talk with other people whenever we are thinking about a new doctor or auto repair shop or when taking trips or going to a new restaurant. We don't think twice about asking people who have been there what they have experienced. We have no doubt that if you were going to spend a lot of money adding a new addition to your house, you would take the

Exhibit 13-2. Two roads to travel—informal and formal.

INFORMAL

METHOD	PATTERN	RESULT
Friend to friend	Unrestricted flow of information	Insightful comments and observations
Manager to manager	Not controlled	Very valuable
Employee to employee	Avoids company policy	
OPEN ROAD—SOME DETOURS		

FORMAL

METHOD	PATTERN	RESULT
Personnel department to personnel department	Very limited amount of information	Little or no information
Company to company	Rigidly controlled per company policy	Limited value
ROADBLOCKS		

time to speak with others to see how well the contractor performed for them. It's just the sensible thing to do.

THE REAL WORLD

Many people when contacted will ignore the company policy of not giving out reference information about a past employee. We can tell you as experienced reference checkers that people want to provide information about someone they know, no matter if they were a good or poor performer. You just need to give them a good reason and make it easy for them to do so. When we contact references, we are able to get cooperation about 95 percent of the time. No more than one in twenty fails to respond or help at all. Although the rules of the game set by most companies forbid talking about someone's personality and performance, most people will not play this game.

If one of your company's executives were to meet an executive from another company at a local restaurant and he was asked his opinion about someone who used to work at your company, do you think the executive from your company would respond that he can't say anything due to your nondisclosure policy? Would he make the other executive contact someone in human resources? If one of your supervisors meets a supervisor from another company at the bowling alley (where they are both on company-sponsored teams) and is asked about a former employee of yours he is thinking of hiring, do you think your supervisor will cite company policy and tell him to call personnel? If you do, you are suffering from a bad case of naiveté and have lost touch with the real world. The overwhelming majority of people will be honest with you if asked the right questions.

There are three basic premises that apply to business and hiring:

1. The chances are overwhelming that a person will not:
   - Perform any better
   - Work any harder
   - Behave any differently for you than he or she has done for others in the past
2. The most powerful tool in business is information

because good managers, given good information, can make good decisions. When making an all-important hiring decision, you need the best information you can get.

3. In the long run, instincts are no match for information. There is a no-more-certain recipe for disaster than a decision based on emotions.

The most progressive HR executives agree on the importance of checking an applicant's background and that this issue cannot be ignored any longer. As businesses nationwide struggle with this situation, many are finding that with creativity and persistence effective background checking is possible. A positive attitude about checking references, coupled with good techniques, will produce wondrous results.

WHY GIVE REFERENCES?

There are good business and commonsense reasons for giving reference information about former employees. Yet, we are amazed at how often these reasons are ignored or overlooked, even by HR professionals and business managers who should know better. These reasons include:

ϙ *Giving references continues company-paid outplacement assistance.* Companies paying for expensive outplacement assistance for a former employee who was fired or released due to downsizing often won't cooperate with another employer who may be interested in hiring this person. We know of a company that was paying in the range of $20,000 for outplacement assistance for one of its separated executives, but would not provide any information about the individual. Paying for professional help and then hindering the process when the unemployed person's job-seeking efforts start coming together hardly makes sense.

৭ *It lowers unemployment costs.* Unemployment rates in most states are based on how long former employees are unemployed and have been drawing unemployment assistance. The quicker these individuals get back to work, the lower your unemployment tax rate will be, so why not cooperate fully with a new employer who may put the unemployed person back into the workforce?

৭ *It ends an unpleasant situation.* When someone leaves or is terminated, for whatever reason, it is difficult emotionally on everyone involved. Unemployed people are often not happy and tend to look backward, blaming their last employer for not fully appreciating or using their talents. The previous employer is trying to get on with business and let bygones be bygones. The easiest way to make this happen is to help ex-employees to find new jobs.

৭ *It provides a reward for good performance and a penalty for poor performance.* Let's suppose someone who worked for you over the past ten years was a loyal, productive, and reliable employee who always received top performance ratings; however, she had to be released when the company reorganized. Another employee, who was employed approximately the same amount of time but had a bad attitude, low productivity, and high absenteeism, was also let go, which was something you had wanted to do for a long time anyway. If someone were to call you about these two people, and under your company policy you aren't allowed to say anything, it could be concluded that both had the same level of performance. The top employee does not receive any credit for being good and the marginal employee is not penalized for her poor work record. Now, wouldn't that be unfair?

Reference-Checking Techniques

BY NOW WE'RE SURE WE have convinced you why it makes sense to choose the references you want to speak with during the interview and not to rely only on the ones the candidate suggests you contact. There is no law that limits your contacts to references that the applicant has listed or has given you permission to speak with. Additionally, you can also develop new references from the references you do contact.

INITIAL CONTACT

When making your initial contact with a reference, take immediate control to ensure that the time spent by both you and the reference is not wasted but instead produces meaningful information. The first inclination of the person may be to not participate in the reference contact. This is because, for years, there has been a negative legal aura that has surrounded reference checking, and there is the resulting fear that you can get into trouble and possibly be sued for what you say.

There is an almost instinctive fear about serving as a

reference for someone who is looking for a job. Most people would just as soon not get involved in a discussion about someone they know for fear that what they say might get back to that person.

The way to start your reference contact is to tell the person that the candidate (by name) has asked (if that's the case) or authorized you to contact him or her as a personal reference in order to obtain a new job. The term *personal reference* is a trigger that usually gets someone's instant cooperation and makes him or her feel more comfortable speaking with you. For help in visualizing this introductory sequence, please note the accompanying work script in Exhibit 14-1.

It is important to remember that when you call people on the telephone, you are interrupting them at some point in their daily activities, so you must try to adjust to where they are at the moment.

All of us have a scale of emotions we go through in a given day, ranging from being happy to being stressed out, and everywhere in between. You will be making contact with a reference somewhere along this emotional scale, and you won't know where beforehand. For example, if the person you contact has just come out of a difficult meeting with her boss, she may be nervous and not fully focused on your call. On the other hand, if she just came out of the boss's office after receiving a big raise, you will probably have a much more cooperative reference. You will be catching everyone along some point in the emotional continuum, and you must learn to adjust quickly.

Another problem you may encounter is that the person you are contacting is busy working on a project or trying to meet a deadline. Your call is an interruption and nuisance no matter how much the person may want to help you and the candidate. You can lessen the feeling of intrusion simply by asking for permission to talk with the reference. For example, you can say:

Exhibit 14-1. Introduce yourself with impact.

If reference answers:
૬ Mr./Ms. _____, my name is _____ and I'm with XYZ Company.
૬ We are in the process of hiring _____. And before we will extend an offer, we need to check his/her background.
૬ He/she has asked that we contact you as his/her *personal reference*.
OR
૬ He/she has given us approval to speak with you as his/her *personal reference*.
૬ I would like to spend a few minutes with you. Is this a convenient time to talk? If not, when would be the best time/day? At work/home?
૬ I will call you then.
OR
૬ I will look forward to your call. Thank you.
If reference is not in:
૬ This is a personal call. When will he/she be in?
૬ Please have him/her call me at _____.
OR
૬ A friend of his/hers has given him/her as a personal reference and I need to speak with him/her as soon as possible. When should I call him/her?
If reference will not cooperate:
૬ Would you like the candidate to call you and personally authorize you to speak with me?
૬ Should I assume that your unwillingness to speak with me means that it would be a bad reference?
૬ Does your refusal to talk about the candidate apply only to this person or to all former employees?
૬ I must explain that unless we can talk with people who know the applicant, there may not be a job offer.
Fallback (comment):
૬ I can't understand why we're having a problem getting you to talk with us, because we're just trying to help _____ get a new job. Whom can I talk with to clear up this matter?

1. "I will need about twenty minutes of your time. Is this a good time for you?"
2. "With your permission, I will ask you a few short questions."
3. "I've obviously caught you at the wrong time. When would be a better time to talk?"

The worst thing a reference will say is, "I just don't have the time right now." But since you've asked permission and have basically put the person on the spot, he or she will more than likely answer affirmatively or will advise you of a better time to call. If the person picks another time to call back, you must be organized and record this telephone appointment in your tickler file. If references state that they cannot provide you with information about the candidate because of company policy, there are methods of obtaining information from these individuals, which will be discussed later in this chapter.

If you call the reference at the appointed time and she tries to beg off your telephone conversation, gently remind her that she said she would talk with you at this time. If she still wishes to end the conversation, you can try rescheduling it. By asking permission, you've transferred the decision to the reference, and you are more likely to be successful.

Getting sufficient time to speak with a reference is a frequent problem. A typical reference call may last ten to forty-five minutes, a significant slice out of someone's workday. Therefore, it may be necessary or advisable to call references at home during the evening or over a weekend to get the information you want. There is usually a noticeable difference in the way people respond when they're at home. They are more natural and relaxed and can give you the uninterrupted time you need to discuss the candidate in question. Most people at work are under heavy time pressure and may also be afraid of being overheard. They may feel that because they are speaking with you while they are at work, they are representing the company rather than speaking personally about the candidate, whereas if they speak with you from the comfort of their home, they are speaking with you more as a personal reference. You don't get good responses when someone's mind is somewhere else. Therefore, you need to eliminate all the distractions that you possibly can.

Occasionally, we have spoken with references at work and then had to finish the conversation after they returned home. It's almost like talking with two different people. At home, people are more responsive to our questions and are often more willing to elaborate. It's always better to have too much time rather than not enough. In our reference-checking practice, we make about 30 percent of our calls after working hours and on weekends to people at home. We don't hesitate to call anyone at home whether it is in the evening, on the weekend, or during a holiday— and have never run into any resentment over our calls.

Now, we realize that people who work a normal workday cannot spend their evenings and free time contacting references. However, in special cases and for critical openings, it may be important to make that sacrifice for your company. An employment manager at one of our seminars explained that because these calls are so much more effective, she encourages her staff members to make after-hours reference calls, and gives them compensating time off for doing so. She added that she can always tell whether they put in the necessary time by the content of the reports they submit to her.

Remember that when you contact someone to be a reference, this person is doing you a favor. Be courteous at all times. Also, be sure that *you* are in the proper emotional state, because if you're upset, you won't see things as clearly.

The following rules may help you to reach your goal of getting a reference to cooperate with you:

1. *Expect the most from all the references you call.* Remember, you are sincerely trying to see your company and the candidate come together. Be absolutely surprised when someone does not cooperate.
2. *Be relaxed, calm, and courteous.* Remember that you are asking someone to give you his or her valuable time.
3. *Explain the purpose of the call.* Tell the reference that an offer cannot be made until references are checked, and that the candidate has asked or authorized you to talk with him.
4. *Ask permission to continue the call.* Inform the reference, "I will need about ten (or twenty) minutes of your time. Is this a good time to talk?"
5. *Expand your information.* Start with verification questions before moving on to performance, developmental concerns, and networking questions, which are covered in more detail in Chapter 15. Continually probe to gain insight.
6. *Don't assume anything.* Listen reflectively and ask for clarification and intent. Understand exactly what the reference is telling you. It's much better to have too much information than not enough.

UNCOOPERATIVE REFERENCES

If a reference is hesitant about speaking with you, explain that a job offer will not be made until you can verify the candidate's background. In most cases, this is all you need to say to get the reference's full cooperation. If this approach does not work, ask him if he would like a personal call from the candidate authorizing him to speak with you. We find that most people agree to start talking after we make this statement. The reference will usually tell you that this won't be necessary because he doesn't want either to bother the candidate or to alert him to his reluctance to speak with you.

If a reference is still unwilling to speak with you, tell that person that her unwillingness to speak with you must mean that it would be a bad reference. Then let the reference defend her position. You can further ask whether her refusal to talk about the candidate applies only to this particular candidate or to all former employees.

Another way to find out about past work behavior is to look into the applicant's reason for leaving the company by asking whether he or she is eligible for rehire. Normally, you won't have trouble getting an answer to this request. If the reference says that the candidate is not eligible for rehire, find out whether the company has a policy of not rehiring after someone leaves the company. If the answer to this question is no, ask the reference some simple questions that require only a yes or no response to clarify why the candidate left the company. Some of the questions you might ask would be: "Was there an attendance problem?" "Did he complete his work in a timely manner?" "Did he get along well with his peers, subordinates, and supervisor?" "Did he have the skills necessary to perform the job?" or "Did he have a good attitude on the job?"

The manager of employment at a large financial services company with a number of full-time in-house reference checkers explained her view of this subject. She said the reluctance of people to give references is understandable. In fact, it is against their company's policy to say anything about a current or past employee, except to confirm dates of employment and job title. However, she feels that an effort must be made to find out something and not totally waste the time spent on a reference contact.

She requires her checkers to ask at least one major question: "Would you want this person to ever rejoin the organization?" She thinks that anything other than an affirmative answer raises suspicion. At that time, every effort should be made to prolong the conversation to enable the reference to convey a feeling about the prospective hire, even if he or she does not articulate it. Her view is to make it easy for the reference to give you helpful information about a candidate, even if it is against company policy. Although no approach works all the time, some effort should be made to learn something from the time spent on the telephone with someone. She feels this approach has paid dividends over the years.

As a last resort, you might pressure the person into cooperating by advising the reference that by not speaking with you he could be held legally liable for the candidate not getting the job. Sound far-fetched? It isn't! We have advised people who had a previous employer who would not speak about their employment at the company to consider taking legal action against that employer for interfering with their efforts to get a new job. We think that you may actually see more of this occurring as a reaction to employer nondisclosure policies.

There is always a final fallback position, which involves exclaiming that you cannot understand why you are having a problem getting the reference to speak with you, because all you are trying to do is help someone she knows get a new job. Then ask whom you can speak with to clear up this matter.

THE VOICE'S BODY LANGUAGE

You can often detect enthusiasm or the lack of it if you pay attention to "voice language." What is said obviously is important, but even more important is *how* it is said or what *is not* said. We all know that body language can communicate a person's innermost thoughts to us. Well, the voice does the same thing.

Although talking on the telephone deprives us of visual clues, it makes it easier to detect language and voice clues and to ask direct questions. Also, being on the telephone makes the other person more comfortable. It's much easier for people to talk when they don't have to face you.

When checking references, never assume anything. If you are not sure of something, continue to probe until you feel that you are being told everything you need to know about the subject in question and that you understand it thoroughly. If you do not understand something, continue to ask questions until you can actually visualize the answer you are being given. If the information is not forthcoming, ask for more information or clarification, with follow-up questions such as, "Would you please give me some examples of his accomplishments in that area?" "Please explain that further," or "I'm having a hard time understanding what you're telling me." Ask follow-up questions in your own language and style. The point is to not stop asking questions until you are sure that you totally understand what you are being told. Above all, do not allow yourself to be "snowed" or misled about a candidate's real qualities and qualifications. We cannot overemphasize the importance of clarifying any information that you do not fully understand.

MAKE IT ENJOYABLE

When calling people, you need to make it easy and enjoyable for both you and your respondent. In our reference-checking practice, we call all over the country and throughout the world. There is a large map of the United States on the wall in front of our desks and a world map, with time zones, on another wall. When we call a particular location, we mentally travel to that spot on the map. We may ask briefly about local happenings or the weather, or if we have traveled there, we may relay our experiences, thereby taking advantage of our chance to speak with someone who is there. We have found that by doing this, the reference often becomes more at ease in speaking with us and is willing to take the time to speak more candidly about the candidate. We truly believe this makes us more enjoyable and interesting callers.

RETURNING YOUR CALLS

How do you get references to return your calls? What you generally must deal with here are voice mail messages and gatekeepers who shield references from you. There is no 100 percent, surefire way to reach people who are not in or are unavailable, but there are a few things you can do to increase your chances.

Leaving a Voice Message

Be prepared to leave a telephone message. Know exactly what you are going to say. Leaving a strong, articulate message will create a positive impression and will probably earn you a return call. A weak, bumbling message will create a negative impression and may stop a return call. Be strong but friendly in your message. This will serve to warm up the reference once you make voice contact. Also, be persistent. If you leave a message in the morning, do not be afraid to leave another message in the afternoon. We cannot tell you how many times references have said to us that they misplaced our telephone number, or have apologized for not getting back sooner but they have been in meetings or may have been traveling.

Leave a voice message something like this: "Mr. Brown, this is Sally Cole with XYZ Company. The reason I'm calling is that someone you know has given you as a personal reference for employment. [*If the applicant is no longer employed there, you may want to give his actual name.*] Please call me at [*your telephone number*]. You may call me collect, if you wish. The time/date is [_____]. I need to speak with you at your earliest convenience. Again, my telephone number is [_____]. I look forward to speaking with you. Thank you."

Dealing with a Gatekeeper

If an assistant answers, you should leave a message similar to the one just given. This assistant is your way of reaching the reference. Make the screener feel important. Sometimes you will find that he or she also knows the applicant and thereby becomes an additional reference contact. You may even get valuable information from this contact, which the original reference may not reveal. Do not let this opportunity pass without learning something. If you reach a real person, not just a recording, ask questions. Treat the gatekeeper with the same courtesy, professionalism, good humor, and sincerity you would use with the reference.

Voice mail and gatekeepers are in maximum use during regular business hours. Try calling before or after work hours, or on weekends. The reference may be working then, answering his or her own telephone. You will find that the higher up you go within an organization, the nicer and easier the references are to speak with.

In short, be creative, make your point, and relay the message you want to leave. Of course, if you are using the new system of your applicant having the references call you, then you won't have these contact problems.

NOBODY'S TALKING

What happens when, no matter how hard you try, you just cannot get people to talk about a job candidate? Do you give up and take the position—which many line managers and employment specialists take—that because checking references is so difficult and usually doesn't work, it should be abandoned as part of the employment process? Absolutely not!

With a little extra initiative, you can make reference checking work for you and get the information you need to make a proper hiring decision. The following actions should help:

1. *Expand (and raise) your contact level.* If you do not want in-depth information about someone, call the HR department. Its job is to enforce the company's no-information policy. A personnel department usually won't give you anything beyond the former employee's dates of employment, previous job title, and possibly confirmation of the last salary earned, sometimes doing this only with a signed release from the candidate. In many cases, HR staff members never worked with the candidate and probably never even met him or her. You know at the outset that this may happen, so do not be surprised by the information you receive.

Obviously, what you must do is expand your contacts to key members of the company who have worked with the candidate. These can be subordinates, peers, or supervisors. We can tell you from years of experience that this is all you need to do, and the higher these people are in the organization, the easier they are to talk to. In fact, upper managers act as if they don't even know that there is a company policy against giving out information about former employees or those who currently work for the company. In most instances, they will freely discuss and comment on the strengths and weaknesses of the person in question in a courteous and helpful way.

2. *Make use of high-level executives.* Upper managers instinctively know that the exchange of information is a vital aspect of business life; they also sense that there are good business and commonsense reasons for giving references. Obviously, you need to make sure you are contacting people who either personally know or have worked closely with the candidate, but that is the only limitation you have. Do not call the chairperson of a company about everyone who has ever worked there; however, do call him or her if the candidate reported directly, or even indirectly, to him or her.

The former president of a small company, which was sold to an overseas organization and dissolved, mentioned in one of our seminars that he personally told his twenty key employees to feel free to use him as a reference when attempting to land a new job. He was surprised that he had only received one telephone call regarding a former member of the company. We can assure you that high-level people are always willing to help someone get ahead. They fully recognize the need for exchanging information. We can guarantee that they have gotten where they are in their careers because others were willing to speak about them.

In fact, when we have problems with personnel staff specialists or line managers who do not want to cooperate, we frequently call the top HR officer and explain our dilemma. Almost without exception, he or she will direct us by name to someone within the company. When we call that person, we mention who suggested that we contact her, and she is then willing to talk.

3. Check your own employees. You may be surprised to learn how often you have employees who know or have worked with the candidate. During the interview, when the candidate is willing to tell you anything you want to hear, ask whether he knows anyone who works at your company. Write down their names. Especially if you're with a large company, you may have all the reference contacts you need without needing to make an outside call. Some companies have added a special section on their employment application form where employees who know the candidate can be identified (see Exhibit 14-2).

4. Confront the candidate. What if information just is not flowing back to you, but you are still interested in a certain applicant? Go back and advise the candidate that you have a problem; that you cannot offer her a job until you have satisfactorily checked her references; and that unless something can be worked out, she will not get the position. Then, together with her, identify references and determine how to get them to speak with you. As mentioned earlier, have her do the work for you in tracking down and inducing these people to talk with you. A good candidate will welcome that role.

LETTERS OF RECOMMENDATION

Letters of recommendation are becoming increasingly unreliable as a means of evaluating job candidates. In almost

Exhibit 14-2. Contacts within the hiring company form.

Do you know anyone employed by the company?	☐ Yes ☐ No
If yes, give name of employee(s):	

all cases, a letter is favorable, even when the writer knows the candidate is mediocre or unqualified. How many negative letters of reference have you seen? Probably not many, because the writer knows the candidate will read the letter and perhaps even sue if the contents are not to his or her liking or are insufficiently substantiated.

When checking references, do not rely on these written documents as proof of the applicant's qualifications and performance on the job. The letter was probably written at the time of termination, and the employer, feeling bad about it, laid on the praise. Also, such a letter can be faked. Contact the person who signed the letter as a reference. You can question her about what was written in the letter to verify that the applicant really did perform as stated.

Let's say that one of your employees has decided to relocate to another part of the country. Because he does not know what companies he will be applying to, he asks you for a letter addressed "To whom it may concern" to attach to his résumé. You can now do one of three things: (1) write a glowing reference, sign it, and send him on his way; (2) ask him to write the letter, then review it, change a few minor points, and return it; or, more advisably (3), tell him that a reference letter is too impersonal and that you'd much rather talk with prospective employers so you can tailor your comments to their job requirements. There really is no better way to give reliable information about a candidate than to speak personally with the prospective employer.

WHEN YOU DISCOVER SOMETHING BAD

Let's take the case where you have spoken with a number of references about a candidate, and then during a conversation with another reference, a point of concern is brought up about him. For example, you call the first reference and he says that the candidate was a good worker and does not indicate that there were any special problems or concerns with the applicant's overall performance on the job. You speak with reference number two, and she basically says the same things as reference number one. However, when you contact reference number three, she states that the candidate was absent from work a lot, which may have been caused by a chemical abuse problem for which he eventually underwent treatment. Now most reference checkers would immediately think that they should contact additional references to get a handle on this issue—which you could do.

However, there is another way to check out "new" information. Since you have already established a telephone relationship with the two earlier references, why not call them back, remind them of your initial contact, and tell them that something has come up since your first conversation on which you need to get their views? Then explain the issue to them. Now that they know you have been made aware of a problem with the candidate, they usually feel a sense of relief because they were not the ones that initially informed you of the problem. You'll be surprised how quickly these references will tune in and try to help you. In a way, you are testing their basic credibility. Contacting references for a second time to clarify questionable information that has subsequently become known is a sensible, yet underused, reference-contact method.

NETWORKING REFERENCES

References will lead you to other references. Normally, you will start with the references the candidate gave you or, preferably, with the references you have identified during the interview as people you want to speak with about the candidate. This is the inner circle of people close to the candidate with whom the candidate may have spoken and perhaps even prepped as to what they should say. However, these references can lead you to the neutrals, that is, people who will freely express their views—good or bad—about the candidate. And they, in turn, may even point out detractors, people who do not like or get along with the candidate.

The way to get this to happen is simply to ask at the end of each reference contact whether the reference can think of or recommend anyone else with whom you should speak. That is all there is to it, and it works. It is nothing more than the simple networking of your reference contacts. Then, of course, based on the particular situation, you decide whether you want to make the additional contacts.

Networking references is the most effective way to go after the special information you want or to keep from being blindsided by a prearranged reference. And, as you have seen, there is no law in any state that says you are allowed to speak only with the references the candidate has given you. You can continue the process for as long as you feel it is necessary.

Some recruiters even ask whether there is anyone the candidate does not want contacted, and his or her reasons for not wanting such individuals approached. Exhibit 14-3 illustrates such a request, which you may want to add to your employment application form.

"Don't Call My Employer"

In our national seminars, the question is always asked, "What do I do when the candidate is currently employed and I can't call his employer because it will jeopardize his

Exhibit 14-3. "Do not contact" form.

At our discretion, we will be contacting people you have worked with in the past.

Is there any reference(s) you do not wish us to contact? If so, please explain why.	DO NOT CONTACT
	Name _____ Reason _____ _____
	Name _____ Reason _____ _____

present job?" Any time someone is in the job market, he is taking a calculated risk that his current employer may find out that he is looking. However, you certainly do not want to do anything that would jeopardize his current job.

The solution is easy. With the candidate, identify people he or she worked with at the company who are no longer there, such as those who have recently left for new employment or who have recently retired. Every company has some turnover. There are also customers, clients, and even vendors who can be contacted. Additionally, you would be surprised how often fellow employees—and even the person's supervisor—know he is looking for a new job. If you ask the candidate, he should be able to supply the names of fellow employees who can be relied on not to spill the beans.

The use of former employees or retirees as references is an excellent practice today. Companies have unloaded thousands of people who can readily be contacted. Because they are no longer connected with the company, they are usually more than willing to talk freely and openly about someone with whom they used to work. We find that we are contacting these people more often as references; in fact, in some cases, they have been our primary source of reference contacts. Retirees will often talk your arm off, because you are talking with them about their old job and comrades, subjects that are usually near and dear to them.

There is never a reason not to check someone's references. Do not ignore your reference-checking responsibility just because someone is currently employed and does not want her current employer contacted. With a little initiative on your part, the situation can be properly handled.

A Personal View

Remember, every reference is a "personal" reference because everyone you speak with knows the candidate personally. As mentioned earlier, to be effective you must talk with references on a person-to-person basis. None of them will give you the official company position on someone they know; however, they can certainly give you their personal view.

The best way to get a person-to-person connection is to stress, when introducing yourself, that the candidate has named him or her as a personal reference, if that is the case, or that the candidate has authorized you to talk with his or her personal references. Everyone you speak with knows the candidate personally, and they are speaking only for themselves.

When you talk to a reference, take your time, ask questions, and listen carefully to what is said. You can usually tell whether the reference is honest and sincere by the responses you receive. Look for the following points:

- What is the reference's real relationship with the applicant (that is, former employer or supervisor, coworker or acquaintance, friend or detractor)?

ᛩ Is the reference professional and well spoken?
ᛩ Does the reference explain his or her answers to your questions?
ᛩ Do you feel that the reference is being truthful or is he or she just saying what you want to hear?

PERSONAL REFERENCES

Many employment specialists advise against using references provided by the applicant, because they are most likely to be friends of the applicant who have been programmed to say only favorable things. We don't agree with this line of thinking and believe that these people can be valuable sources of information for the following reasons:

ᛩ *Most people do not want to get involved in lying, even to help a friend.* We are convinced that, with a few exceptions, people are not comfortable lying and certainly do not want to lie for someone else. If you ask the right questions, they will be honest with you. In fact, we have actually had personal references named by the candidate tell us that something the candidate said was false or badly misleading. Even personal friends often go out of their way to set the record straight.

ᛩ *Personal references are usually not prepared for unexpected questions.* No matter how well rehearsed a personal reference is, he or she will not have an answer ready for every probing question a good reference checker will ask.

ᛩ *Personal references will lead you to the neutrals and the detractors.* References can quickly take you to other people who also know the candidate, even to those who do not think highly of him or her.

ᛩ *Personal references can provide special information about the applicant.* Sometimes, there is an important concern about the candidate that needs to be cleared up, such as instability, bad habits, or family difficulties. We have frequently been asked to try to determine whether an applicant still has a chemical-dependency problem. When speaking with his or her friends, we find that they will be frank in discussing this issue. Moreover, if you are preparing to relocate someone to a new part of the country, you should explore how friends think this will affect the candidate's family situation.

> We performed a reference check for a major company that was preparing to hire a young woman who had a high-paying job in San Francisco. She was willing to work in a small city at a much lower salary. Talking with her friends, we quickly discovered that she was dating a young medical doctor in the new town and fully expected that they would be married soon—and wanted to concentrate her full attention on this relationship. With this information in hand, her willingness to move and take a decrease in salary made a lot of sense.

TELEPHONE TIPS

We strongly suggest trying what we call the "exact-time" method for calling people, which we have used with great results. This involves, whenever possible, establishing an exact time to speak with a reference and then calling back at precisely that time. In other words, when you call someone or make a return call, advise the person of the specific time that you will call. Tell the reference, or the person scheduling the calls, you will call at a certain time, emphasizing that when the telephone rings at that time, it will be you.

You would be surprised how often the person we have set up an exact time with is literally sitting by the telephone waiting for the call. However, there have been a few times when, for some unavoidable reason, we were not able to make the call at the time promised. When we called back later, we were told that the irritated person was sitting by the telephone or had altered his or her schedule in anticipation of the call. After profusely apologizing for our mistake, we then proceeded with our reference call.

The exact-time method will save a lot of time and reduce your frustrations with having to play telephone tag. It also shows references that you are willing to work within their schedules to make it more convenient for them. Try it for all your calls, business and personal.

REFERENCES BY MAIL, BY TELEPHONE, OR IN PERSON

The best way to gather background information about someone is to visit the reference and have a face-to-face discussion. However, from a practical standpoint, that is not possible. It takes a lot of time and money.

The next best, and most practical, way is to use the telephone to contact references using the practices and techniques outlined in this book.

In our view, the least effective way of checking references is to write letters. It is both time-consuming and seldom produces information. Those companies and people who do it by mail are probably more administrative minded than results oriented, or, as one seminar participant said, they are taking the cowardly way to perform their background-checking responsibility.

Efforts to check the applicant's background by mail may be futile. Previous employers may be slow in answering queries received through the mail, or they may not answer at all. Studies have shown that the return rate can be as high as 56 percent and as low as 18 percent. The reason for the overall low return rate is that many employers are concerned that former employees may take them to court over information written on a reference form.

Another problem is that it takes too long, usually two to three weeks, to receive a reply. If you are trying to hire in job categories where candidates are in short supply, applicants just won't wait for you to go through this long and involved process.

You are far better off checking references by telephone. You will receive comprehensive information, while spending less time and effort. However, when searching the public records outlined in Chapter 11, you may need to use the mail, fax, or Internet.

Reference Checklists
and Questions

ASKING THE RIGHT QUESTIONS IS more than half the battle in gathering reference information. Every question asked during a reference call makes a statement about how good you are at what you're doing. The quality and depth of your questions will ultimately determine the quality of the answers you receive.

You, as the questioner, should always remain in control during the course of the conversation. The person who talks may monopolize the conversation; however, the person who asks the questions will control the conversation.

Checking references is a time-consuming task that can be performed by the hiring manager or an employment specialist. However, because of workload pressure on these individuals, you may prefer to hire an outside firm that specializes in reference checking. Professional reference checkers can uncover a great deal of information at a reasonable cost. A word of caution: Do not delegate this task to a low-level employee who is untrained in checking references. This type of employee will not learn much and can even embarrass the company.

CONDUCTING THE REFERENCE CHECK

We recommend that you always start your reference checking with education. We have found that about one out of ten job candidates inflates or falsifies his or her education level. With few exceptions, this information can be easily verified over the telephone. If you find a discrepancy in the candidate's education, you may not want to proceed any further. However, if you are interested in the candidate, at least you'll already be alert to the possibility of fraud.

We have found that one of the major problems most companies face in gathering outside reference information are their telephone questionnaire forms. In most instances, these forms are simple generic-type checklists that are used for all reference contacts, regardless of the position applied for. In addition, such forms usually contain numerous questions and allow little room for writing. Some forms even contain boxes to check off the answer. These forms obviously do not allow you to ask in-depth questions and can also be stressful to use.

Exhibits 15-1 through 15-4 are sample reference checklists to help guide you in calling references. There is a separate sheet for each type of reference contact—business, personal, or customer—as well as one for hourly employees. These have been uniquely designed to be different for each type of contact because the flow of questions varies. The questions in these sample forms were predesigned for the type of reference being contacted.

Note that these reference-calling forms are laid out differently from the ones used by most companies. In these, the questions are on the left-hand side; the right side serves as a work space. When information is coming in quickly, it is necessary to be able to write freely, to draw arrows connecting related information, or to circle important facts. It is much easier and more natural than trying to fill in the blank spaces on a tightly printed form.

In one of our seminars, a woman pointed out that this made a lot of sense to her. She had been using a yellow pad next to her company's reference-checking form to give her plenty of room to write. She then transferred the information onto her checklist when she had the time. Any method that involves rewriting the information gleaned is inefficient and time-consuming.

When calling references, the flow of questions must be right. For this reason, the placement and wording of the questions on our sample calling forms have been tested and retested to maximize their effectiveness.

The checklists start with simple verification questions, then move on to performance-related information, then to developmental opinions, and finally to networking your reference contacts. We have tried whenever possible to use indirect questions—that is, questions that get the desired information without requiring the reference to give a personal opinion or explanation. Note that there is a space in each question to use the applicant's name.

The business reference checklist (see Exhibit 15-1) warrants special explanation because it is the one you will probably use the most. Let's look at what we consider to be key questions on this checklist, and why we have found them to be so useful.

Question No. 9: "Have you seen [John's] current résumé? Let me read you what it says were his duties and accomplishments at your organization."

One of our favorite stories involves a situation where it was suspected that the applicant's résumé was not entirely accurate. As the résumé was being read to the reference, the only response given was hysterical laughter. Finally, after reading the ten-sentence description on the résumé, the reference said that he wanted to get his su-

(Text continues on page 196)

Exhibit 15-1. Business reference checklist.

BUSINESS REFERENCE CHECKLIST

Candidate	Person Contacted
Potential Position	Position: _____
Job: _____	Company: _____
Company: _____	Location: _____
	Bus. Tel.: _____
	Home Tel.: _____

VERIFICATION

1. I'd like to verify _____ dates of employment from _____ to _____.
2. What type of work did _____ do? (Title/general duties?)
3. Were _____ earnings $_____ per _____? Were there any bonus or incentive plans?
4. Why did _____ leave your organization?

PERFORMANCE

5. What do you feel are _____ strong points on the job? What characteristics do you most admire about him/her?
6. Did _____ supervise other people? How many? How effectively? Can he/she create team effort?

7. What are _____
   shortcomings? Was
   there anything he/she
   was trying to change
   about himself/herself, or
   should be trying to improve on?

8. How would you rate
   _____ overall
   job performance on a
   scale of 1 to 10 (10
   being high) compared
   with others you ob-
   served in a similar ca-
   pacity?

9. Have you seen _____
   current résumé? Let me
   read to you what it says
   were his/her duties and
   accomplishments at
   your organization.

10. Is _____
    honest?

11. How well does
    _____ relate to
    other people? Which
    employees does he/she
    work best with: Superi-
    ors/peers/subordinates?
    Is he/she a team player?

12. How did _____
    last job performance re-
    view go? What strengths
    were cited? What rec-
    ommended improve-
    ment areas were noted?

(continues)

Exhibit 15-1. (*continued*)

How about the perfor-
mance review prior to
that?

13. What do you feel
were _____'s
most major accomplish-
ments with your com-
pany? What changed as
a result of his/her
involvement?

14. On average, how
many times did _____
miss work or come in
late? Does he/she have
any personal problems
or bad habits that inter-
fered with his/her job
performance?

15. Whom did _____ work
for prior to joining your
company? When hired
were his/her references
checked? What did the
references have to say?

DEVELOPMENTAL

16. What is the biggest
change you've observed
in _____? Where
has there been the most
growth or development?

17. Is _____ in the
right job/career? How
far do you think he/she
can go?

18. What do you feel frustrated _____ in his/her last position with your company?

19. How did _____ handle himself/herself in times of conflict?

20. If _____ asked you what one thing would most improve the way he/she performs on the job, what specific advice would you give him/her?

21. What is the best way to work with _____ to quickly maximize his/her talents and effectiveness for the company?

NETWORKING

22. What other person(s) know _____?

Name: _____   Name: _____
Title: _____   Title: _____
Location: _____ Location: _____
Telephone: _____ Telephone: _____

OVERALL RATING:
   Excellent ☐   Good ☐   Some Reservation ☐   Poor ☐
Check made by: _____ Date: _____
Comments/Summary:

pervisor. When the supervisor came on the line and the résumé was reread, you could now hear two people laughing uncontrollably. When asked what they were finding so funny, the supervisor said that what had actually been read was a description of his (the supervisor's) job and the résumé was completely inaccurate. He further commented, "If he was that good we would have hired him for my job."

If you remember nothing else from this book, remember this technique. If you suspect the candidate's résumé is inflated or wrong, read it to the reference. This has worked innumerable times in our reference-checking practice and for other people who have used it. If there is an error or lie on the résumé, the reference will tip you off by his or her reaction and will then proceed to tell you how the résumé should read. You can also use this technique when someone refuses to give you reference information. Ask whether you can at least read what the applicant said on his or her résumé. Usually, the reference will consent and then make valuable comments about what is stated on the résumé.

Question No. 12: "How did [John's] last job performance review go? What strengths were cited? What recommended improvement areas were noted? How about the performance review prior to that?"

Why try to reinvent the wheel? If you're talking to the applicant's previous supervisor, rather than asking for an opinion about the candidate, why not have him or her relay what was reported on the last performance review? It doesn't require any new judgment or opinion, so there should be much less resistance to providing this information. Ask if the employee was given a copy of the performance report. If so, you may want to have him bring it in for your personal review.

Question No. 20: "If [John] asked you what one thing

would most improve the way he performs on the job, what specific advice would you give him?"

You can usually sense when the reference does not want to say something unfavorable about the candidate. However, we have found that this question helps to uncover more information. You will find that the references are usually open, helpful, and honest in answering this question.

The personal reference checklist (see Exhibit 15-2) is for use with someone who knows the candidate only on a personal basis, but has not worked with him. It is self-explanatory and appropriate for this type of relationship.

The customer reference checklist (see Exhibit 15-3) is for contacting someone whom a sales applicant has called on. The questions fit this type of business relationship and will produce valuable information.

The hourly employee reference checklist (see Exhibit 15-4) is designed specifically for reference contacts on hourly employees. This checklist was designed for a major client of ours who wanted to get quick and meaningful information when hiring someone to work in the company's plants. Once you've established contact with the reference, it takes only about five or ten minutes to get this basic information.

In Exhibit 15-5, there is a separate form entitled Reference-Checking Questions (short version), which corresponds to the form entitled Interview Questions (short form) in Exhibit 8-5 in Chapter 8. The match between questions on these two different forms makes for quick and efficient reference checking.

The more information you ask for, the more you will get. And if you don't ask, you don't get. It is that simple. We often receive positive feedback on these questions. It is not unusual for references to make such comments as, "That's a good question," or "You are really making me

Exhibit 15-2. Personal reference checklist.

PERSONAL REFERENCE CHECKLIST

Candidate	Person Contacted
Potential Position	Position: _____
Job: _____	Company: _____
Company: _____	Location: _____
	Bus. Tel.: _____
	Home Tel.: _____

VERIFICATION

1. How long have you known _____?

2. What is his/her relationship to you?

3. How often do you see _____?

PERFORMANCE

4. Have you ever worked on a committee or been involved in any organizations with _____?

5. What was _____ position in this committee or organization? How effective was he/she?

6. What is your opinion of _____ character, dependability, and general reputation?

7. What strengths do you feel _____ will bring to the position he/she has applied for?

8. Are you aware of any personal trait or skill that _____ is trying to improve?

9. What basic values does _____ hold for himself/herself?

10. Do you feel _____ is honest? Has there ever been any evidence to the contrary?

11. Does _____ have any personal problems or bad habits that you have ever noticed?

12. Why do you feel _____ has applied for this position?

DEVELOPMENTAL

13. What is the biggest change you've observed in _____? Where has there been the most growth or development?

NETWORKING

14. What other person(s) know _____?

(continues)

Exhibit 15-2. (*continued*)

Name: _____   Name: _____
Title: _____   Title: _____
Location: _____   Location: _____
Telephone: _____   Telephone: _____

OVERALL RATING:
   Excellent ☐   Good ☐   Some Reservation ☐   Poor ☐
Check made by: _____ Date: _____
Comments/Summary:

think," or "I'm writing that question down to use my-self."

PEELING THE ONION

Let's imagine that references are an onion with many layers. When you first start out your conversation with a reference, you are basically talking to the outermost layer, which contains very little information. The actual information you want this reference to provide is located in the layers underneath, and you must peel this onion layer by layer to obtain the information you are seeking.

The following scenario is an illustration of this point:

You ask a reference, "How was Matt's attendance?" and the reference replies, "It was good."

At this point, because the answer was not necessarily derogatory and the reference did not point out any problems, you may be inclined to go to your next question regarding Matt's skills on the job. However, you have only engaged in a superficial level of the conversation. You've been held to the outer part of the onion and are still far from the truth.

Exhibit 15-3. Customer reference checklist.

CUSTOMER REFERENCE CHECKLIST

Candidate

Potential Position

Job: _____

Company: _____

Person Contacted

Position: _____
Company: _____
Location: _____
Bus. Tel.: _____
Home Tel.: _____

VERIFICATION

1. How long did _____ call on you? Did he/she open your account?
2. How often did _____ visit or call?

PERFORMANCE

3. What type of product or service was _____ selling?
4. How would you describe _____ sales style compared with other salespeople who were calling on you?
5. How was _____ knowledge of the product or service he/she was selling? Did he/she present the product or service in a positive manner?
6. Was _____ able to solve problems in a timely manner?

(continues)

Exhibit 15-3. (*continued*)

7. Did _____ keep you abreast of what was happening in the industry?

8. Were you satisfied with the way _____ serviced your account?

9. What did _____ do that pleased you? Displeased you?

10. Compared with the average salesperson, how would you describe _____ level of professionalism?

11. If _____ were to be calling on you again with another company, would you be pleased/displeased/neutral?

12. Is _____ honest? Any evidence to the contrary?

13. Does _____ have any personal problems or bad habits that you have noticed?

DEVELOPMENTAL

14. What is the biggest change you've observed in _____? Where has he/she grown the most?

15. Is _____ in the
    right job/career? How
    far do you think he/she
    can go?

NETWORKING

16. Who else knows
    _____?

Name: _____   Name: _____
Title: _____   Title: _____
Location: _____ Location: _____
Telephone: _____ Telephone: _____

OVERALL RATING:
  Excellent ☐   Good ☐   Some Reservation ☐   Poor ☐
Check made by: _____ Date: _____
Comments/Summary:

Now it may be true that Matt's attendance was
"good" in comparison with others', but what does that
answer really mean? This type of a response does not give
you enough information to go on, does it? You need to
peel back that first layer and direct the conversation to a
deeper level.

The way to get deeper and more meaningful information is quite simple: Just question the answer to your previous question or ask for further clarification. So, when
the reference says, "It was good," you ask, "How many
times was Matt absent or late in the past year?" The reference pauses a moment and responds, "Well, he probably
missed a couple of days a month and was late about once
a week."

Now you have received more detailed and relevant

Exhibit 15-4. Hourly employee reference checklist.

HOURLY EMPLOYEE REFERENCE CHECKLIST

Candidate	Person Contacted
Potential Position	Position: _____
Job: _____	Company: _____
Company: _____	Location: _____
	Bus. Tel.: _____
	Home Tel.: _____

VERIFICATION

1. _____ said that he/she worked for you from _____ to _____. Is this correct?
2. What type of work did _____ do? (Title, general duties?)
3. Were _____ earnings $ _____ per _____? Were there any bonus or incentive plans?

PERFORMANCE

4. How often did you observe _____ on the job?
5. How was _____ attitude on the job?
6. How was _____ attendance? How often was he/she late or absent?

7. Is _____ hon-
   est? Any evidence to the
   contrary?
8. How well did _____
   fit in and work with
   others?
9. What do you feel were
   _____ strengths
   on the job? What areas
   of improvement would
   you recommend?
10. Were there any special
    skills that _____
    were required to have in
    order to perform his/her
    job?
11. How productive was
    _____? How
    high are his/her quality
    standards?
12. How much supervision
    does _____ re-
    quire? How fast does he/
    she learn?
13. Why did _____
    leave the company?
    Would you rehire him/
    her?

OVERALL RATING:
  Excellent ☐   Good ☐   Some Reservation ☐   Poor ☐
Check made by: _____ Date: _____
Comments/Summary:

Exhibit 15-5. Reference-checking questions (short version).

You have selected someone you are enthusiastic about. Now verify that what you have been led to believe is in fact true and accurate. Use these key questions for all the references you contact about the candidate.

- ও How long did _____ work for your company? Why did he/she leave? [*Go back at least five to ten years.*]
- ও Specifically, what did _____ do for you?
- ও What were _____ accomplishments? What changed as a result of his/her being employed there?
- ও What are _____ strengths as you see them? Would other people agree with you?
- ও What other people (supervisors, coworkers, subordinates) can I call about _____? [*Get at least one name.*]
- ও What do you feel separates _____ from others doing the same or a similar job?
- ও What can we expect from _____ if he/she comes to work for us?

A final word of advice: Use common sense, as you would for any kind of decision. Look for solid evidence that the person you choose is, in fact, the person who can increase your in-house capabilities and really help your operation.

---

information that could help you in your hiring decision, but it is still not deep enough. So, you respond, "Were you happy with Matt's attendance?" The reference replies, "No, I talked to him several times about improving his attendance." You then ask, "Was there any improvement in his attendance record?" The reference replies, "Whenever I talked to him, he would get better for a while but then would slip back into his old ways."

At this point, you have penetrated to a deeper layer of truth—a level that can make a real difference. You now have excellent information on which to base your all-important hiring decision.

Compare that to the reference's superficial reply, which you may have been tempted to accept. But you chose to dig deeper with a second question. Finally, at the third level, you sought and got a truly significant answer.

Getting to the deeper layers of truth is not easy. It requires a certain skill in asking questions and you must develop the courage to dig for the answers even though it is easier to accept what you're told and move on. The benefits of "peeling away the onion," however, are well worth the effort.

All successful reference checkers ask a series of questions to encourage the reference to reveal critical information about the candidate. When they are given negative information, they then probe deeper, by asking more questions, to find out how this impacted the candidate's performance and others on the job. Do not be afraid to keep peeling back the layers until you fully understand what you are being told.

It has been our experience in supervising, training, and working with hiring managers and employment specialists that they generally do not look deep enough. The majority will stop pursuing information after the first question, and thereby see only the onion's surface. A small number will ask a second-level question, but very few will consistently probe further to get to the heart of the onion, where the truth really lies.

The reference will not simply volunteer the critical information. Getting to level three, or to the heart of the matter, takes persistence.

SOME GOOD TIPS

Here are some useful techniques you can use:

❧ *Look for extremes and their opposing sides.* For example, the biggest flaw that many aggressive people have is that they tend to take on more tasks than they can handle and end up dropping the ball on many of them. Or they may not be sensitive to the needs of others. Another example would be workaholics, many of whom have not learned how to delegate properly. Any time you note an overwhelming strength, turn the coin over and see what you find. In many of us, our biggest strength is also our biggest weakness.

❧ *If a reference you call just won't cooperate in any way, there is one last fallback technique that can make your call worthwhile.* Describe the new company and the job the candidate will be performing. Ask the reference for his opinion as to whether this position sounds right for the applicant. You will be surprised how often the person will give you his or her view on this question. Then, at least, your time has been productive rather than wasted.

❧ *Read back what the reference has said on certain points to make sure you understand exactly what was meant.* Oftentimes, references will provide additional information or clarification. We started using this technique after a number of references asked us to read back to them what they had told us to verify that we were both on the same page. They wanted to be sure of the accuracy of our interpretation and our listening skills and thoroughness. This technique ensures the reference that you understood and have properly recorded the information being provided.

Handling the Rejected Applicant

WE BELIEVE THAT HANDLING A rejected applicant is a misunderstood subject that needs to be examined more thoroughly. Saying the right thing to a candidate who is not going to get the job is critical because your words will leave a lasting impression about you and the company. And, what you say and how you say it can also prevent a hiring discrimination charge. In our many years in the employment business, we have seen more confusion on how to handle the rejected applicant than on any other aspect of the employment process.

BEFORE THE DECISION

First, let's look at how to advise candidates, after you have interviewed them, that they are not strong contenders for the job opening. All too often, because we do not want to hurt the job applicant's feelings, we try to sugarcoat the rejection in the hope that we will both feel better about the whole situation. Many interviewers will tell all the candidates that they are in the running and thus keep everyone up in the air. The problem with this nice-guy technique—which is a form of avoidance—is that some applicants will take this to mean that they are viable candidates. They will falsely get their hopes up and may even stop interviewing with other employers. To avoid this scenario, we suggest that you tell the candidate in whom you no longer have an interest, something like this: "You are a fine candidate and we appreciate your taking the time to talk with us. However, we are talking with other qualified people and you should certainly continue your interviewing activity."

Above all, always let the applicant leave the interview feeling positive about your company. Looking for a job is never easy, so make the visit with you as painless and pleasant as possible. Whatever you do, treat the applicant with respect and courtesy.

AFTER THE DECISION

Then there is the applicant who knows he was a finalist, but for whatever reason—sometimes bad references— failed to get the job. Never divulge or try to explain the factors that went into your decision, because you may not know all of them yourself and it can only cause trouble. Above all, never tell the candidate that your decision was the result of derogatory information received from the references you contacted. This is both dangerous and unnecessary. Do yourself and the candidate a favor: Get on with your business, and let the candidate get on with his or her life. We suggest you advise the finalist in whom you no longer have an interest along these lines: "It was very, very close, and certainly a difficult decision for us to make, but we decided that another candidate more closely meets our needs at this time." Do not, under any circumstances, go beyond this basic explanation. In fact, just keep repeating it to the job candidate as often as you need to.

However, with this new system of having the candidate contact and set up the reference calls, the applicant may surmise that she apparently did not make it because of what the references said or because of other derogatory information learned during the background review. Again, stand firm and use the statement suggested previously. Do not disclose any more information than necessary.

File your reference notes and reports separately. A personnel record should not include employee references supplied to an employer if the identity of the person making the reference would be disclosed. What we recommend is that after you have made your hiring decision, you keep only the records required by law. If you are not required to keep a record—then get rid of it. A perfectly innocent document can be made to look sinister in the hands of a skillful investigator or attorney.

If you are ever tempted to violate these rules—in the belief that you are only being helpful—by telling someone in specific terms why he or she did not get the job, do not do it. You could end up spending weeks defending yourself, your company, and even your references from the complex inquisition of a rejected job candidate. When it is all over, no one has gained—especially not the candidate or you.

We recall a story in this regard that clearly illustrates the damage that can be done to everyone concerned. A job candidate couldn't understand why he did not get the job because from what he could tell, everything in the hiring process seemed to be going his way. He asked the employment manager and was told that the president of the company had instructed not to hire him. The candidate immediately insisted on seeing the president, causing much disruption and embarrassment in the process. As a result of this poor handling of an employment rejection, the company terminated both the vice president of human resources and the employment manager.

NOTIFICATION METHODS

There are two considerations regarding the rejected applicant. First, do you notify the candidate yourself or do you wait to see whether he or she contacts you? The most-well-run employment offices try to notify applicants quickly whether they get the job or if someone else was selected. Much depends on the volume of your employment operation. Second, do you call the applicant on the telephone or do you send a letter to the rejected candidate? Giving notice of rejection by telephone can be time consuming and awkward for both parties. Most employment offices seem to prefer sending a letter to the person. A rejection letter provides clear documentation of the decision and ends the relationship. A form letter (see Exhibit 16-1) is usually the quickest and best way to handle this difficult issue. Send the letter promptly to avoid telephone calls or visits by the applicant. Then mark or note the final contact in the applicant's file, before closing the matter.

If you're involved in hiring people and want to be good at it, you must learn how to handle the rejected applicant properly. We firmly believe that this is an area where you are able to quickly distinguish between the true professional and an unprepared amateur—however well intentioned.

Exhibit 16-1. Rejection letter.

[*Date*]

[*Applicant's Name*]

[*Address*]

[*City, State, Zip*]

Dear [*Applicant's Name*],

It was a pleasure meeting with you on [*date*] to discuss possible employment with our company. I was impressed with your credentials and gave careful consideration to your application.

However, we have selected an individual we feel more closely suits the needs of the position at this time.

We thank you for your interest in our company and sincerely wish you the best of luck in your future endeavors.

Regards,

[*Your Name*]

Part V Summary

In Part V, you learned that:

ॱ By using the right questions and techniques, you will get good results.

ॱ People basically want to help another person to get a new job and will be honest about someone they know or have worked with.

ॱ To get correct and insightful information about someone you might hire, you must ask questions. Do not hesitate to continually probe to better understand what someone is saying.

ॱ You must understand and recognize the current situation of all the references you contact to get their full cooperation and honesty.

ॱ You should never provide an applicant with the reason he or she was not selected for the job. Advise the candidate that someone else was selected and leave it at that.

VI

Creativity—The Key to Success

Improving
Performance in Your
Organization

ONE OF THE MAIN REASONS for writing this book is that we feel HR professionals need to be bolder in their recruiting efforts and have often failed to perform diligently in their work. In our view, they would have done themselves a far greater service had they figured out sensible ways to exchange job performance data with each other about current or past employees rather than devising ingenious excuses as to why the necessary background information could not be obtained.

It seems we have lost sight of the practical side of hiring people. There is no substitute for common sense when picking the right person for your organization, and we suspect that most executives would agree with us. Is checking the background of a candidate a good investment? The trouble caused when you are forced to fire someone who does not work out after a few months makes the up-front investment next time look quite smart. Let the good ones come to work for you and let the bad ones

217

go to work for your competitor! You can and will win the hiring game by using common sense and the effective reference-checking techniques outlined in this book.

The 80/20 Rule
We have found that the 80/20 rule applies to virtually every organization:
80 percent of your problems come from
20 percent of your employees.
SO
One-fifth of those you hire will cause most of your future difficulties.
THEREFORE
It makes sense to identify who they are—and not hire them.

The single biggest mistake a manager can make is a bad hire. And yet, they are made all the time. However, an effective preemployment screening program can reduce hiring mistakes by at least 75 percent or more.

You will build a far better workforce if you follow the ideas discussed in this book. Exhibit 17-1 summarizes the principal lessons taught here. Follow these points carefully to build a trouble-free workforce. Don't let your learning lead to knowledge alone. Let your learning lead to action and results.

REFERENCE CHECKING PAYS OFF!

Attracting and hiring the best workers is crucial to building your management team. If you do not hire the right people, it will directly affect your productivity and bottom line.

An employee's past is a look into his or her future. A thorough review of a potential hire's history will give you

Exhibit 17-1. Building a trouble-free workforce.

Assumptions:

ᖾ The chances are overwhelming that a person will not perform any better, or work any harder, or behave differently for you than he or she has for others in the past.

ᖾ Eighty percent of your problems will come from 20 percent of the people you hire.

ᖾ You should not hire anyone who has been a problem for someone else.

Finding the Right Employee:

ᖾ Decide to validate that what you have been led to believe about a candidate is, in fact, true and accurate (the key).

ᖾ Announce to each candidate that total honesty is expected and that references will be checked (scare tactic).

ᖾ Ask probing questions during the interview (check honesty). Identify by name the key people (above/same level/below) in the candidate's work life (develop references).

ᖾ Tell the candidate to have certain references you have selected call you, or to set an exact time for you to call them (save time and effort).

ᖾ Question references and diligently verify the information you have received. They will tell you, or at least signal to you, whether the individual has been a problem to them (spot liars and troublemakers).

The Result:

ᖾ Avoid a hiring mistake by knowing the full truth about the applicant. Start with the right people. Build a trouble-free workforce.

---

the blueprint you need for gauging that individual's future performance. If history repeats itself, then choose your history carefully. Careful reference checking can uncover patterns of behavior that do not show up on an application form, on a résumé, or in an interview.

A company we have worked with started checking references on all job candidates before extending any offer of employment. It kept records for a full year, before and after checking references, with the following results:

	Control Year	2nd Year*
Number of candidates interviewed	168	153
Number of finalists	44	38
Number of reference checks completed	0	38
Number hired	29	22
Number hired who then left the company	16	2

*After reference checks had been instituted.

Did their reference-checking efforts pay off? The company had a much-higher-caliber workforce and a greatly reduced turnover. It also had better production figures and less friction among employees, and in the long run, it had to spend far less time hiring new people.

Pre-employment reference checking should be seen as an aggressive, proactive way to reduce turnover and build a high-quality workforce. It is more than simply a way to limit legal liability. It can have a great impact on the bottom line.

Good hiring becomes self-perpetuating because your own employees will refer their friends to your company. Good people know other good people, just as bad people know other bad people. Hiring the right people will make your company a winner all the way around. Reference checking pays . . . and pays . . . and pays.

APPLIED CREATIVITY

It's time for what we call *applied creativity*—that is, creativity that rolls up its sleeves and gets to work. It is a form of creativity that can lead to quantum leaps in improving your overall hiring process.

It has become necessary to validate through others what applicants believe or say about themselves. Only by having an in-depth discussion with those individuals who have been closely associated with the candidate, in a working environment, is a true evaluation possible. Information about an applicant's previous work experience and overall performance on the job is absolutely critical for a smart hiring decision.

A word of caution: It is natural for an employment specialist or a hiring manager to become biased toward the top candidate and possibly lose his objectivity regarding the person. For example, the lead HR representative designated to recruit and hire an advertising director at a company we are familiar with also had the responsibility of checking the references of the final selection. The reference check signaled that there might be a problem with the candidate's integrity that required further evaluation. However, the employment staff member responsible apparently overlooked this negative information and concluded the search was "successful." When the new employee did not work out due to honesty issues, the hiring process was carefully reviewed and the system was changed. A separate individual, with no stake in the search, was assigned to perform the reference checks.

This provided a greater degree of objectivity and impartiality in the reference-checking phase of hiring.

The recruitment process is a long and time-consuming task, depending on the level of the opening to be filled. In a typical recruiting effort, about 25 percent of the time is spent searching for candidates, about 30 percent on screening replies and résumés, 35 percent on interviewing, and at least 10 percent (ideally) on checking references. That is a full hiring sequence, and making it a winning process requires sound application and creativity.

NETWORKING

An increasing number of companies are networking with each other regarding the hiring of people. Every one of you has a counterpart at every company for which a job applicant has ever worked. Why not call that individual and ask for information, perhaps off the record, about the candidate? We guarantee that in most cases, even though you have never met the person with whom you are speaking, that person will provide you with information about someone you are about to hire. Yet, very few of you will do this.

Your counterpart in the profession can be an enormous asset, even if that person works for a competitor. Let it be known that you will return the favor when needed. It is amazing how effective this can be and it is used all the time in business. Salespeople build networks of contacts as a way to prospect for new business. Executives belong to the same clubs in order to socialize and exchange thinking. Managers play golf with other managers from different companies. It is all part of the way business is conducted. HR members can take a similar approach to prospect for new employees and to obtain informal feedback about candidates being considered. Co-operative relationships with counterparts in other companies can be an invaluable help and source of information when the effort is made. When we bring up this subject at seminars or when we advise employment specialists how to be more effective in this regard, we are amazed at how often it seems like a new thought or approach; yet, everyone agrees that it makes sense. Let's face it, when one hand washes the other, they both get cleaner.

It is time for the HR function to be bolder and more results oriented, instead of trying to invent reasons or procedures to keep something from working. If you're not networking to fill yourself in on the backgrounds of potential employees, you are missing the boat.

> We cannot overemphasize the value of networking when checking out job candidates. A large company we are familiar with hired a top-level research executive who was offered an elaborate employment contract, costly relocation provisions, and other expensive perks to entice him to change jobs. After he had been on the new job a short time, it became obvious that he was not qualified for the position. He had severe personality problems and was not getting along well with others in his group. He also lacked the necessary technical abilities and was not showing up for work on time. He was obviously a poor choice, and everyone in the company was wondering why this person had been hired. Finally, the CEO of the new company took action and called his counterpart, the CEO of the employee's former company. He was quickly told that this individual's performance on the job had been slipping badly for several years, quite noticeably in his last few months. In fact, they were ready to terminate him when the new company hired him. The CEO of the former company went on to say, "We couldn't believe our good fortune

> when we heard you were hiring him. You not only solved
> the problem of terminating him but you also saved us a
> lot of money in severance pay." He went on to say that
> he would have been glad to tell someone in the proper
> position what was going on, but was never contacted.
> Needless to say, the company CEO called in the appro-
> priate staff members and informed them about what he
> had been told and asked why no effort had been made
> to contact the former employer about someone they
> were putting into such a key position in the company.
> To make a long story short, the vice president of HR was
> reprimanded and shortly thereafter resigned, while the
> director of professional staffing was fired. There just was
> no excuse for making an important and costly company
> decision without doing the necessary background re-
> view.

When it comes to hiring and exchanging information about former employees, it is almost as if companies are at war with each other. This antipathy needs to be stopped for the good of our own companies and those fine people who need a job.

OUTSOURCE SCREENING TASKS

Trying to verify the credentials and checking the background of job applicants is a time-consuming task and headache for most managers. Although some HR professionals believe that an employer should call a candidate's references personally, others prefer the objectivity and timesaving benefits offered by an outside firm. Also, some feel that when you have been involved with the candidate, you may not be impartial or objective in checking him or her out.

Many employers use an outside professional service to perform part or all of their preemployment screening.

These firms are experts at checking the backgrounds of prospective employees, and they understand the legal and regulatory aspects of hiring. Professional screening firms are located throughout the country. Some are quite large, while others may be small operations with a few employees. Some have been around for a long time, and some are brand new.

Selecting the right vendor from the many that are available can be a complicated exercise. The basic considerations are the cost of the service rendered; the response or turnaround time; and, most important, the quality of the information provided. The less expensive service is not always the best—and you usually get what you pay for.

We suggest you look at the following major points when selecting an outside employment screening service: the length of time in business, the level and strength of its customer referrals, the expertise and experience of staff members, and its hours of operation and availability for your time zone. Also, will the vendor help to guide the company's hiring policies and actions to comply fully with federal and state employment laws and regulations?

The bottom line is whether the service firm can match its claims. If your company does not have the personnel or the time to do the necessary screening and searching, by all means consider outsourcing some or all of these responsibilities. The employer has the right and duty to do everything possible to ensure that the individual being hired is, in fact, the right person for the job and the company. A small up-front investment can be money well spent.

Companywide Hiring Standards

MOST ORGANIZATIONS NEED TO STRENGTHEN their review of job applicants, as well as improve applicants' understanding of the company's expectations. A standardized form should be used to ensure that all units verify applicants' references and educational level, and possibly credit history and police record. Reference checking should not be limited only to those people listed by the applicants. Documentation should include who was contacted, the date, and a signature of who conducted the check.

A companywide policy should be implemented that specifies which company positions require credit checks, criminal checks, or driving reviews. We suggest that new hires have at least a criminal records check and that credit checks be considered for new hires who will have access to cash or large financial transactions and all senior-level administrative positions. Orientation of new employees should include information about company policies and procedures related to fraud and theft, as well as a means for new hires to acknowledge that they have received the information.

A company's internal audit, general counsel, and HR offices should monitor the program. Each company location should have some freedom as to the process and the procedures, but the basic requirements should be met and carried out properly.

ADVICE TO HUMAN RESOURCES PROFESSIONALS

For those working in HR departments, remember: You're not simply managing a major function of your company; you're influencing the organization's future by the people you choose to hire. The old personnel department has undergone a dramatic change over the past twenty-five years, evolving from strictly an administrative unit to one of the most important areas of business. Employees represent a company's biggest line item expense—with the largest and most regular cash flow outlay—as well as its greatest asset. The hiring decisions you make have a very positive or negative effect on the organization's success.

It is time to rethink the entire hiring process and to explore new alternatives. It is time for HR professionals to do everything legally possible to ensure that they are hiring the right people. In today's complex and confusing world, it has become necessary to stay on the cutting edge of hiring—become proactive, not reactive—with respect to tracking a person's background. In order to make your job easier and to get you started right away, we have provided an abbreviated lesson in Appendix A, entitled Process Summary and Sample Telephone Script.

IN CONCLUSION

There is no question that today's job applicants often fabricate or exaggerate their previous experience or past performance. As a result, employers must be on guard and alert during the entire hiring process.

Whether considering a management or production employee, you need to ensure that the candidate will fit into your company. The best way to do this is through effective reference checking.

Conducting a background check on a potential employee can be difficult, and there are legal complications. But the bottom line is that an employer has the legal right and need to ask a candidate about his or her prior employment and to call his or her previous employers or associates.

Many companies and individuals think that there are legal restraints against talking about past employees or associates because of past interpretations and misconceptions on the subject. As a result, special measures and techniques may be necessary to be successful in this area.

It is important to get the necessary information from others concerning a candidate's accomplishments and other important data to make an informed hiring decision. Convincing former supervisors and others to disclose information about a candidate's past performance and strengths or liabilities is a necessary component in the hiring process.

The candidate can be used to track and locate the references with whom you would like to speak. By asking the candidate to provide the documentation and information you need, you can be successful in obtaining information about his or her past performance. A person's past performance is a good indication of how well that person will perform in the future.

The amount of information that can be obtained depends on the reference checker's skill in communicating with references, usually by telephone. The primary tools are a reference-checking form and good listening skills. It is important to ask the same questions for each reference and to record the information received. Being prepared in advance is the key to success in this endeavor.

The background-checking process has two parts. The first is determining the candidate's past history and performance record. This may include dates of employment, job title, salary and accomplishments, plus personality factors. This information is normally obtained from the people for whom the candidate has worked, those who may have worked under or around the person, and possibly friends and acquaintances. A direct conversation is necessary to obtain this information. The second level of information involves facts about the candidate such as level of education, credit standing, police record, and licenses held. This can be obtained by contacting the appropriate office where the information is on file. Overall, you want to gather an honest description of the candidate.

The best references are past supervisors, subordinates, and coworkers—and in that order. They can give an accurate assessment of the person when on the job. The candidate can help to identify and locate the proper individuals. It may also be valuable to network references to find other people who have seen the candidate in real-life situations. It is best to speak with a cross-section of references to obtain a balanced view of the candidate and to get behind any differences of opinion.

Almost without exception, it is best to check only the final candidate for the opening as determined by your screening process. In other words, learn all you can from interviewing the available applicants, make your decision as to who you feel is best suited for the position, and then check the references to validate that what you have been led to believe about that person is, in fact, true and accurate. Reference checking is time-consuming and should not be used as a screening method.

It is important that the person doing the reference checking knows what to expect and how to handle and communicate with references. This is a vital function, for both the organization and the candidate, and should be handled professionally, whether done in-house or by an outside firm.

Repeated surveys have shown that people often lie about their background and accomplishments, and sometimes about who they actually are. Hiring the wrong person can be a costly mistake to a company. Good reference checking has become a necessity in today's world of rapidly changing standards and expectations.

The most underused source in reference checking is, in fact, the candidate. He or she can identify and locate references and clear up any confusing or derogatory observations. By working with the candidate, if necessary, clarification can be obtained and mistakes avoided.

As a reference checker, you will be calling strangers who do not know you and may not even know your company. Also, you will be asking for their valuable time and personal attention, and to participate in something that may make them apprehensive. If the candidate has notified the references that you will be calling, they will be expecting your call and the process should go much more easily.

Your discussions may provide information that will lead you to check further regarding some part of the candidate's background or qualifications. This may require that you contact additional references or it may lead you to eliminate the candidate from further consideration. It is important to build rapport with the references quickly, so that they feel comfortable enough with you to be honest.

Overall, checking references properly is well worth the time and effort. Placing the right people in the right jobs should be the goal of any well-run employment function. The long-term success of the organization may depend on how well this is carried out.

In this book, we believe that we have covered the subject of background screening from A to Z and from every angle. We are confident that you will find new or improved ways and means to be a more effective HR manager or hiring representative for your organization. Best wishes in your changing and challenging role. If you have any comments or suggestions, please write to us at Certified Reference Checking, Co., 2977 Highway K-PMB 112, O'Fallon (St. Louis), Missouri 63366-0291. We would like to hear from you.

Appendix A

Process Summary and Sample Telephone Script

IF THE CANDIDATE HAS DONE his or her job, the reference will be expecting your telephone call. This should make it easier to start the conversation and to maintain an open and friendly exchange of information.

STEP 1: MAKE ADVANCE PREPARATIONS

Always have the appropriate questions prepared in advance for the level of the position to be filled (managerial, professional, or customer) and the type of reference (personal or business related) as discussed and shown in Chapter 15 (see Exhibits 15-1 through 15-5). It is important to use the right set of questions that match the opening and the person being spoken with. Know in advance the exact questions you plan to use and ask basically the same questions for all the references spoken with.

As you develop your questions in advance, think about the requirements of the job. Ask questions that will provide the information you need as well as confirm your opinions concerning the candidate.

STEP 2: CONTACT THE REFERENCE

Identify yourself, your organization, and the nature of your call, which is to verify information provided by the candidate. You may want to briefly describe the position to be filled. Assure the reference that everything that is discussed will be treated confidentially.

If the reference hesitates, find out the reason and address the problem. Let the reference know that an offer will not be extended until you have been able to speak with people who have worked with or know the candidate. If this is not an appropriate time, set a time to call back even if it is at the reference's home.

The telephone reference check is essentially an interview with the reference. The key is to be friendly and relaxed. Your best chance of getting the information hinges on your advance preparation, confidence, persistence, and assertiveness. Always speak with a smile in your voice. Address the reference by name and include the candidate's name when asking questions.

STEP 3: OBTAIN INFORMATION FROM THE REFERENCE

Always start out by verifying the basic information provided by the candidate, such as dates of employment, job title, duties performed, reason for leaving, and salary. Always start the reference check with easy questions that only call for factual or yes or no answers. Starting with difficult or opinion-oriented questions can quickly derail the conversation.

Be prepared to handle resistance. References are often reluctant to share information or to tell you what you need to know. There is almost an inborn fear that they may say something illegal or damaging against the candidate. Keep your questions and discussion neutral so that you do not upset the reference. For example, you might ask something like this, "How does Jim/Jill handle pressure?" or "How did Jim/Jill handle pressure on the job?" Avoid questions like, "Did Jim/Jill ever fly off the handle?" or "Was there anyone Jim/Jill didn't get along with?" The correct choice of words is critical.

As you speak with the references, you may encounter inconsistent information. You may find varying views and opinions about the candidate. Whenever you find inconsistencies about the candidate, it behooves you to check further and to go back to references you have already spoken with or to contact additional references to clarify the information you have obtained. Of course, you can also speak with the candidate and see what he or she says about the incident or problem. In any event, whenever you discover inconsistencies, find out through further questioning what really happened or what is actually correct.

Questions that would be illegal to ask candidates during the interview are also illegal to ask a reference (see Chapter 7 for an in-depth discussion of this area). All questions should be job related, and there must be consistency in what you ask each reference. If you ask different questions, you will not be able to properly compare the replies received.

There are certain general questions and areas that should be explored for practically all potential new hires. Among these are:

- Reason for leaving current or last job
- Exact position held
- Overall work performance
- The candidate's strengths and weaknesses
- Areas where improvement was needed

ᛉ Ability to communicate when speaking and in writing

ᛉ Ability to get along with others

ᛉ The quality and quantity of work performed

ᛉ Eligibility for rehire

ᛉ A rating of the person's overall work performance compared with other similar employees

ᛉ Any special problem areas or reservations about the person's ability to perform the job for which the person has applied

STEP 4: OBTAIN ADDITIONAL BACKGROUND INFORMATION

Depending on the position being filled, you may want to also conduct one or more of the following checks on the candidate: educational attainment, credit report, civil court records, driving record, workers compensation claims, and criminal records going back ten years. This may be done concurrently with the reference checks, or before or after the reference-checking phase. It is suggested that the educational check be conducted first because it is quick and an area where there is a high amount of falsification, in which case you may not want to proceed further. See Chapter 11 for a full explanation of where and how information of record is obtained.

SAMPLE TELEPHONE SCRIPT

The following is an example of a successful telephone reference check:

Caller: "Good afternoon. My name is Jane Smith and I'm with ABC Company. The reason I am calling is because John Doe has given you as a personal reference for new employment with our company as a senior accountant. Is this a convenient time to talk?" *(See Chapter 14, specifically Exhibit 14-1, for how to introduce yourself with impact.)*

Reference: "Yes, I have a few minutes. I know Mr. Doe very well and would be happy to speak with you about him." *(If the time is not convenient, arrange a future time to talk.)*

Caller: "Mr. Doe indicates that he has worked at your company since October 1999 to the present as an auditor, and that you are his current supervisor there."

Reference: "The dates sound accurate, although I do not have his file in front of me to give you John's exact date of employment. You could contact our human resources department if you need this information. However, John has reported to me for about two years and has done a good job for our company."

Caller: "John said that his current salary is about $40,000 per year?"

Reference: "Yes that's accurate.

Caller: "Having worked with John for the last couple of years, what do you feel are his major strengths on the job? In other words, how well does he perform the requirements of his job, and does he get the results?"

Reference: "I think John is one of our best auditors. We have six full-time auditors and he clearly stands out as one of the best. He knows accounting and financial controls, and he understands operational matters. He has been especially helpful to a number of our plants in identifying and correcting some serious and persistent problems. He establishes good rapport with the auditees and is well respected. John is the person many people within the company come to for assistance and guidance. In fact, we would like to promote him to audit leader if he stays with us. Personally, I would like to have more people on staff like John. He seems to have it all together."

Caller: "Where do you feel he excels the most?"

Reference: "He is technically strong and he has a good understanding of processes. He is very detail oriented and methodical and is able to develop very good solutions to problems."

Caller: "Everyone has an area where they can improve. If John were to ask you what area he could improve in, what advice would you give him?"

Reference: "Well, John can be tough on his fellow workers who he feels are not carrying their load. He does not hesitate to tell them that they are not giving their all."

Caller: "Has this created any serious problems with those he is working with?"

Reference: "No, not for us. In fact, it shows that he is ready to assume a supervisory position. As I said before, he is very detail and task oriented and he expects others to be the same. Let's face it, as an auditor, you can't afford to let anything slip through the cracks."

Caller: "How would you rate John's overall job performance compared with others you have seen in a similar role? Are we talking about outstanding, above average, or average?"

Reference: "I'd say that on a scale of 1 to 10 (with 10 being high) he's a 9. He's clearly a cut above his peers and it's obvious he enjoys his work. I will hate to lose him. In fact, I'm trying to get him to stay with our company, but, unfortunately, I think he's already made up his mind to move on. He would like to gain more experience."

Caller: "Well, how far do you think John can go in his career? What is his long-range potential?"

Reference: "There's no question that John will be a controller some day. He certainly has the potential to move to the top financial management role in a company.

He's very dedicated to his career and he does not back down from challenges. I think John is on the fast track."

Caller: "How would you describe John's overall attitude and personality?"

Reference: "He is pleasant and well spoken. He knows how to fit in and be accepted. Almost everyone likes John."

Caller: "How about any shortcomings? Is there anything John is trying to change about himself or he should be trying to improve on?"

Reference: "He could probably learn to relax more. He is pretty intense and he needs to learn to be easier on himself. I have pointed this out to him and I feel he has gotten better in this regard. John works a lot of hours and he needs to take more time for himself."

Caller: "Are there any other areas where John should be trying to improve?"

Reference: "John has a tendency to try to impose his thinking on others. His eagerness and aggressive nature can irritate his contemporaries. He needs to change his style somewhat so that he gets better cooperation from others."

Caller: "How does John react in a crisis or difficult situation?"

Reference: "He bears down and tries to find the best solution possible. John almost seems to thrive on difficult situations because it gives him a chance to think and go forward."

Caller: "What do you feel has been John's most major accomplishment at your company?"

Reference: "John has definitely made many significant contributions to our company, but what initially comes to mind is when he corrected a serious problem we were having in our warehouse. He is very computer literate and he found out that our system of tracking was inefficient.

He established new procedures and assisted in implementing a new system that not only helped to track our inventory but also saved a lot of money for the company. We no longer had to worry about having too much inventory on hand."

Caller: "How well does John communicate?"

Reference: "He is very well spoken and his written material is excellent. Also, he is a good presenter in a group situation."

Caller: "Do you feel John is honest?"

Reference: "Absolutely. He has great integrity. I trust him totally."

Caller: "Has John ever had any serious personal problems or bad habits that would have interfered with his job performance?"

Reference: "No, not really. He did go through a nasty divorce and had to take some days off. However, this is now in the past. He lives a clean life and does not drink or smoke."

Caller: "Has John talked with you about why he is willing to leave your company at this time?"

Reference: "Yes, and he told me you would probably be calling. He sees the position with ABC Company as a step up in his career. Also, the salary is better than what we can offer him and there is more growth potential because you are a larger company with a number of operating divisions. I know he would like to get out of auditing due to the large amount of travel that is required. He told me that he is starting to feel somewhat burned out as an auditor."

Caller: "Do you recommend him to a new employer?"

Reference: "Absolutely. Although I know that means that I'm probably going to lose him. He is ready to move on in his career. There's no doubt that you will be getting a very dedicated and responsible individual who will give you a 110 percent effort on the job. Our loss will be your gain."

Caller: "Is there anyone else that you think I should speak with regarding John?"

Reference: "I'm probably the closest to him as his immediate supervisor. There are coworkers and other managers in the company with whom you can speak. But I recommend that you work with John if you want to reach them. I don't think everyone here is aware that he is looking at new opportunities."

Caller: "I really appreciate your time and cooperation. If I need any other information, I will get back to you."

Reference: "Fine, I owe it to John to help in his career plans."

Caller: "Thank you, again. I've enjoyed talking with you. Have a great day!"

Reference: "You do the same. Good-bye."

As you can see from the previous example, the caller started the conversation with the reference by building rapport and asking easy questions. The checker then moved on to the more difficult questions. Of course, this was an example and your questions may be different. However, you should not be satisfied until you feel certain that you have a good picture of the candidate and are comfortable with the information you have.

Always make notes of the responses you receive. As in the interview, it is difficult to keep information straight if you are speaking with a number of candidates. The reference-checking forms should be used and filled out properly.

Be sure that the candidate has signed a separate release giving you permission to talk with people, of your choice, about him or her. (See Exhibit 8-2, Authorization for Release of Information for Employment Purposes.) Also, let the candidate be your helper during the entire endeavor. This can save a great deal of time.

You will be successful in checking references if you follow the lessons and procedures outlined in this book. Also, you will be performing a valuable service for your company.

Appendix B

National Credit-Reporting Agencies

THE THREE NATIONAL CREDIT-REPORTING agencies are Experian, TransUnion, and Equifax, and each could potentially contain different information.

The following list provides the contact information:

- Experian: The telephone number is 888-397-3742, or go online at www.creditexpert.com. The Credit Expert site also gives you the option of ordering a report simultaneously from all three reporting agencies, which saves you steps but costs a few dollars more.
- TransUnion: The number is 800-888-4213. Otherwise, order online at www.transunion.com or by mail at TransUnion LLC, Consumer Disclosure Center, P.O. Box 1000, Chester, PA 19022. If ordering by mail, include first, middle, and last names (including Jr., Sr., III); current address; previous addresses in the past two years, if any; social security number; date of birth; current employer; telephone number; signature; and appropriate fee.
- Equifax: The telephone number is 800-685-1111 or go online at www.equifax.com.

Index

Fair Credit Reporting Act
(FCRA), 1, 52–53, 67,
95, 135, 141–143
family status, asking about,
75
FCRA, *see* Fair Credit Reporting Act
Federal Trade Commission,
142
fingerprinting, 1
firing guidelines, dealing
with, 118
fitness requirements, 74
"fool's gold," 27
Form I-9, *see* Employment
Verification Form

gaps, career, 22
gatekeepers, dealing with,
176–177
G.E.D., verification of, 136
good faith laws, 57, 64
*The Guide to Background In-
vestigations,* 138–140

handwriting analysis, 32
high school diploma, verification of, 136
hiring, negligent, 60, 62
hiring standards, companywide, 226–227
honesty/competency ma-
trix, 24–26
hourly employee reference
checklist, 197,
204–205
human resources (HR) pro-

fessionals, 217, 222–
224, 227

ID cards, 147
identity checks, 147
identity theft, 147
illegal background checks,
4–5
illegal immigrants,
148–149
Immigration and National-
ity Act, 148–149
Immigration Reform and
Control Act of 1986
(IRCA), 67, 149
information
exchanging, with other
HR professionals,
222–224
flow of, 160–161
formal vs. informal gath-
ering of, 160–162
importance of good,
163–164
obtaining, from refer-
ences, 234–236
INS (U.S. Immigration and
Naturalization Ser-
vice), 149
interview(s), 93–110
appearance of candidate
during, 39–41, 94
areas to avoid in, 73–75
asking for examples of
proven job perform-
ance during, 27
asking open-ended ques-
tions in, 73

About the Authors

Edward Andler, a prominent authority on hiring matters, is the founder of Certified Reference Checking Co., a St. Louis–based firm. He is the author of two books on hiring, *Winning the Hiring Game* and the first edition of *The Complete Reference Checking Handbook*.

Andler, a University of Missouri graduate, has spoken and presented seminars on hiring and reference checking throughout the country. *The New York Times* cited him as "the acknowledged dean in his field." Prior to starting his firm in 1988, he was a human resources manager and executive with U.S. Gypsum and General Dynamics. He has also been an executive recruiter and outplacement specialist with two national service firms.

Dara Herbst has been with Certified Reference Checking Co. since 1993, in charge of operations. She is highly regarded for her in-depth knowledge of reference checking at all levels.